THE WIT & WISDOM OF
Lee Kuan Yew
[1923–2015]

EDITORIAL DIRECTOR
Douglas Amrine

EDITOR
Lindsay Davis

RESEARCHERS
Sim Ching Yeng • Jacqueline Eu • Sng Siok Ai • Miriam Ee • Valerie Ho • James Lui

DESIGNERS
Lisa Damayanti • Nelani Jinadasa

PRODUCTION MANAGER
Sin Kam Cheong

PUBLISHED BY
Editions Didier Millet Pte Ltd
35B Boat Quay
Singapore 049824

www.edmbooks.com

ISBN: 978-981-4385-28-2

Jacket image: The Straits Times © Singapore Press Holdings Limited. Reprinted with permission.

First published in 2013

Reprinted in 2015 (two times)

Printed by TWP Sdn. Bhd., Malaysia

THE WIT & WISDOM OF
Lee Kuan Yew
[1923–2015]

edm EDITIONS DIDIER MILLET

CONTENTS

PUBLISHER'S NOTE

Lee Kuan Yew played the pivotal role in Singapore's transition from British Crown Colony to independent developing nation, and on to the economically powerful and diplomatically influential city-state it is today. Throughout this surprising and at times painful journey, he has proved a charismatic and occasionally controversial leader. Lee is a conviction politician whose speeches are unambiguous, characterful and eminently quotable; this collection of almost 600 short quotations provides a compelling summary of his views on a wide range of topics from Singapore's past, present and future.

Lee began his political career while Singapore, having suffered the deprivations of Japanese occupation during World War II, was extricating itself from British control before establishing itself as a separate nation from Malaysia. Racial tensions were high, communism was gaining a foothold in Southeast Asia, and the economic challenges to a small, largely undeveloped island were enormous. Lee's views on the issues of this time still resonate today.

Singapore's ties to Britain continued to be strong, and Lee watched closely as many European countries developed into welfare states. He rejected this economic model out of hand, and spoke forcefully about entrepreneurship, labour relations and economic development.

As Singapore became more developed and affluent, and mass communications connected all the world's peoples, Lee spoke often of the Asian values which he believed gave Singapore an important advantage both socially and economically. Ever conscious of the country's multicultural population, he also spoke from the heart on the benefits and disadvantages of bilingualism.

Lee's pragmatism and unwillingness to be influenced by external pressures characterized his leadership style: "I was never a prisoner of any theory. What guided me were reason and reality. The acid test I applied to every theory or scheme was, would it work?"

Although Lee stepped down as Prime Minister in 1990, his opinions are still keenly sought out in Singapore, in ASEAN and indeed across the globe. Whether he is talking about the environment, corruption, democracy or the world's future, his voice is one that few can ignore.

The quotations found in this book have largely been selected from Lee's public speeches and statements, which have been collected in Singapore's National Archives and the Singapore Parliamentary Record.

ON SINGAPORE

Those of us who sometimes talk of unity and confederation do not understand that Singapore is the shop window of Malaya. This is the little place where people come and do their buying and their selling. This is also the little laboratory where the British, the nationalists and the communists first try out their tactics, because if anything goes wrong, it goes wrong on a small scale.

1956

Before one has a nation, there must be two things. First, the content of a common people with a common identity of interest, a common social experience. And, secondly, complete freedom to exercise the collective will. One may precede the other.

1960

I do not pretend to be able to solve the problem of agricultural land in Singapore. It is one of those problems which are basically unsolvable. If we succeed as the industrial base in Malaysia, as we may well do in the next decade, then there is no place for either grazing land or agricultural land in the popularly understood sense of that term. Singapore is an industrial city, and the price of land is being determined on the basis of a developing industrial complex.

1964

To sit on a stool is more comfortable and stable than to sit on a shooting stick. Right? Now we are on a shooting stick. But I intend to sit on that shooting stick and since that is all that I have got – 214 square miles – we will jolly well make it a strong shooting stick. You have seen Singapore, the people here? It is a shooting stick made of steel.

1965

In other parts of the world, when their pigs suffer from swine fever, they hush it up. They pretend they do not have it. Net result: all pigs get infected, the position becomes permanently chronic. We can do likewise. But we will become permanently a chronic society: sick. So when we get swine fever, we announce it, alert everyone, so that we can arrest the spread of the disease and bring back normalcy. This is what is required of this community: all the time, that push, that thrust to counter the natural sluggishness which this climate tends to build into our physical systems, and all that while, we must have an awareness of the realities of life.   1967

—◦—

We have created this out of nothingness, from 150 souls in a minor fishing village into the biggest metropolis 2 degrees north of the equator. There is only one other civilisation near the equator that ever produced anything worthy of its name. That was in the Yucatan Peninsula – the Mayan Civilisation. There is no other place where human beings were able to surmount the problems of a soporific equatorial climate. You can go along the equator or 2 degrees north of it, and they all sleep after half past two – if they have had a good meal. They do! Otherwise, they must die earlier. It is only in Singapore that they don't. And there are good reason for this. First, good glands, and second, good purpose.   1967

—◦—

Nobody here dies of starvation. Nobody is allowed to beg in streets. When we find someone begging, we put him into a home and feed him. And, in two to three years, with all our cleansing services reorganised, we will make this one of the cleanest and most beautiful cities in Asia with trees, flowers and shrubs in all the public places.   1967

Few countries in Asia or Africa have taken over from European colonial administrations, and improved on what they had. We have been able to do this because we have never been afraid to face up to our problems and to tackle them with vigour.   1968

———◦∞◦———

Between Japan and Europe, we must make Singapore the best place to bunker and repair ships, either in drydock or on water. Once we have established ourselves as the ship repairing and shipbuilding centre, we will remain so for a very long time. For once supremacy has been established, whether it is an airport, a harbour, or a dockyard, it is very difficult for any other place to dislodge us. For others have to compete against an established centre with superior facilities, higher skills and expertise, and long-standing established customers.   1971

———◦∞◦———

Hard-headed industrialists and bankers of developed countries never take unnecessary risks. They look round the world for places where there is political stability and industrial peace before they invest. In Singapore they find such a place. Hence the massive inflow of capital, machinery, technological know-how and banking expertise.   1972

———◦∞◦———

We do not intend to let the population drift away from the city centre because of the high price of land. It would be wasteful to have such a city. We must retain that unique feature of the Singapore that we have known for so long, a city bustling with life from the crack of dawn to past midnight, one which throbs with life and vitality.   1976

———◦∞◦———

We are not Britain. We cannot be Britain. Remember that.   1976

Why do you think pregnant women want to come to Singapore to give birth? Because then the child can become a Singapore citizen, isn't it? Then you are entitled to jobs, schooling, jobs, medical attention – the whole works. Surely, that is a back-handed tribute to the society that we have built up.   1976

———◦———

We can build up this team spirit, this *esprit de corps*, where every individual gives of his best for the team, for the nation, to achieve its maximum. And the team, the nation, in turn, takes care of the individual, fairly and equitably. The art of government is the art of building up team spirit.   1980

———◦———

'Excellence' encapsulates in one word how Singapore can survive in a very competitive world.   1987

———◦———

A society to be successful must maintain a balance between nurturing excellence and encouraging the average to improve. There must be both cooperation and competition between people in the same society. The Singapore cooperation and competition have improved standards of life for all.   1987

———◦———

The past has been a series of immense challenges over survival and deprivation. We have secured our survival although we can never banish danger. We have provided for our basic needs, homes, schools, hospitals and health services, jobs, whatever. But in no case is the standard ideal. In each case the next generation has to improve on what we have done.   1989

In America, New York is the hub of banking and securities activities and over-the-counter derivative products, while Chicago is the exchange-traded derivative centre. In Europe, Zurich is Europe's premier safe haven for funds although London has the bigger financial clout. Singapore has the attributes to be the Chicago and the Zurich of East Asia. We have a record as a safe haven.   1994

—◦◦◦—

We had to make ourselves a small but nevertheless useful part in the international system of the exchange of goods and services, of investments, banking and finance, transportation and communications. If we were no longer relevant to the advanced countries then we would be reduced to agriculture and fishing, and our population would shrink to what it was when the East India Company first came to Singapore to establish a free port – a fishing village of 120 people, living at subsistence level on fishing, root-staples and piracy!   1996

—◦◦◦—

People are not aware of Singapore's vulnerabilities. All they read and see is No. 1 or No. 2 competitive country, No. 1 seaport, No. 1 airport, No. 1 airline, and so on. Sometimes they complain that we are driving people too hard and making life too stressful, so why not settle for No. 2 or 3, or 4! But it does matter, for if we are not near the top in competitiveness, there is no reason why we should have a seaport, or an airport, or an airline – or indeed why there should be a separate independent Singapore. It is as simple as that.   1996

—◦◦◦—

Singapore can act as a 'Partnership Centre' to bring together strategic alliances for companies to invest in third countries in the East Asian region. Besides our familiarity with regional regulatory and market conditions, cultures and business practices, we have a wealth of *guanxi* or human connections.   1996

We are the resource-poorest country in the region, and therefore we cannot afford to be other than honest, efficient and capable if we are to stay out of trouble.   1998

Singapore has survived and prospered by making ourselves relevant to the world. In the last century, we traded in spices; this century, in tin and rubber. After independence in 1965, we moved into simple manufacturing. Now, we are in wafer fabs, pharmaceuticals and Asian currency units. As the world economy changed, so did we.   1999

One arm of my strategy was to make Singapore into an oasis in Southeast Asia, for if we had First World standards, then businessmen and tourists would make us a base for their business and tours of the region.   2000

We faced tremendous odds with an improbable chance of survival. Singapore was not a natural country but man-made, a trading post the British had developed into a nodal point in the worldwide maritime empire. We inherited the island without its hinterland, a heart without a body.   2000

However spectacular the advances in technology permitting point-to-point communications through the internet between someone in Africa and someone in Mongolia, in the end transactions need to move goods and people. Here Singapore has the advantage. We are already one of the global hubs for warehousing, logistics, transportation, communications, banking and financial services. It is not only the world-class infrastructure. More important is the expertise, the software programmes, the Singapore brand name we have built for trustworthiness, efficiency, speed and reliability.   2001

With two huge countries, like India (1 billion) and China (1.3 billion) and Central and Eastern Europe and Soviet Russia (together 0.5 billion) entering the world marketplace, our competitive position has changed. The world has millions of leaner, keener and hungrier workers to compete against us. We can only win a place in this race by being better educated, with higher skills, and by maintaining a more conducive and secure environment for investments, with a government that provides efficiency, security and industrial peace, with fair returns for capital invested. It is the bottom line that counts.

2003

—◦◦◦—

If I were young in my 20s, Singapore is one of the best places to be in. I can get a good education, a solid foundation for life to do best in life. Whether I am Singaporean Chinese, Malay, Indian or whatever, I can get a first-rate education, enjoy excellent health services, good and affordable housing and have a safe environment to bring up children. I can maximise my opportunities by learning English as my first language, keep as much of my Chinese as I can, and learn Malay as my third language so that I can understand what people in Indonesia and Malaysia are saying on TV and in the press. Because English is my master language, my Mandarin can never be equal to that of China's Putonghua, nor do I want to become like one of China's Chinese. Then my value-add to any China Chinese joint venture is zero. With 1,300 million Chinese they do not need another Chinese. It is because I am a Singaporean Chinese with worldwide connections with Americans, Europeans, Japanese, Indians, ASEAN and other peoples, who all use English as the first or second language, so I can add value in any cooperative enterprise with China Chinese. What I need is enough command of Mandarin and understanding of present-day Chinese culture to work easily and comfortably with them. And with Singapore as my home, the world is my oyster, for I can afford to travel anywhere in the world for leisure or business.

2004

I believe the PM and the majority in Cabinet have made the right decision [to allow casinos in Singapore]. To say 'no' after worldwide publicity for a year, Singapore will be sending out the wrong signal, that we want to stay put, to remain the same old Singapore, a neat and tidy place with no chewing gum, no smoking in air-conditioned places, no this, no that – not a fun place.   2005

—◦◦—

Singapore is now a brand name. Singaporeans are sought after in the oil states of the Gulf because they are known to be capable, honest and can work out proper systems. They like the Singapore system and want to adopt parts of it.

2006

—◦◦—

We have made home ownership the cornerstone of Singapore's public housing policy – the vast majority of the population own, not rent, their homes. Ownership is critical because we were an immigrant community with no common history. Our peoples came from many different parts of Asia. Home ownership helped to quickly forge a sense of rootedness in Singapore. It is the foundation upon which nationhood was forged. The pride people have in their homes prevents our estates from turning into slums, which is the fate for public housing in other countries.   2009

ON SINGAPOREANS

Citizenship is essentially a question of loyalty. A man is a citizen of a state and has the right to determine the future of the state because he is part of an entity. It is really a subjective question: Is this my country? Do I owe it undivided loyalty? Am I prepared to fight and die for it, if necessary? But there is no known test yet that you can apply – no known lie detector or psychological machine to record the heartbeats or the brain beats of a man to test this. If there were, then we can scrap all this question of whether it is ten years' residence, whether one speaks a certain language or whether one swears an oath of allegiance or an oath of renunciation. You can go through all these formalities and still have no loyalty to a country.   1957

—∘—

In the university students of today, we must find the administrative, technical and professional talent to man the institutions of state in the near future. If they share an identity of purpose and have common beliefs, then we may succeed in creating a distinct people with a common language, history and political institutions. If not, then we may be bedevilled by all the problems of a multiracial society which achieved political independence before it had acquired a common social identity.   1960

—∘—

If they could have just squeezed us like an orange and squeezed the juice out, I think the juice would have been squeezed out of us, and all the goodness would have been sucked away. But it was a bit harder, wasn't it? It was more like the durian. You try and squeeze it, your hand gets hurt. And so they say, 'Right, throw out the durian.' But inside the durian is a very useful ingredient, high protein.   1965

It is not the individual performance that counts. Of this, I'm quite certain. You can have a great leader, you know. If the herd hasn't got it in it, you can't make the grade. The herd must have the capacity, the stamina, sufficient social cohesiveness to survive. 1965

———⊂o⊃———

I do not want a suppliant, an inert society where people just say, 'yes' to everything I say because that means it is a society with no verve, no vitality. But, at the same time, I expect you to start thinking; not just to mouth old slogans which are no longer relevant. Start thinking. 1966

———⊂o⊃———

One of the by-products of a migrant community is that it produces a population of triers. Whatever else they may lack, the offsprings of migrants are prepared to try anything to improve themselves. Having left tradition, their history, their past behind, they have only the future to go in quest of. 1966

———⊂o⊃———

We have what sociologists call a highly 'achievement-oriented' type of society. For every boy, every girl here tonight, there are fathers and mothers egging them on to perform better than the other pupils in school. Not all societies have this. In many societies, they are quite happy just to sit down under the banyan tree and contemplate their navel. So when there is famine they just die quietly. Here, they will not die quietly. If there is no food they will do something, look for somebody, break open stores, do something, plant something, and if they have to die, they die fighting for the right to live. 1967

———⊂o⊃———

There is tranquillity, poise and confidence in Singapore. And it is a confidence born out of the knowledge that there are very few problems which we cannot overcome, given the framework of honest and effective administration. 1967

I am trying for you. But please remember you must try for yourselves all the time. I can't do the work for you. I can work for you, sometimes 15 hours a day. I ask you to work hard and well, for yourselves, only eight hours of that day.　　　　　　　　　　　　　　　　　　　　　　　　　　1967

———◇◦◇———

This is our first problem: the will to be a people. That we must have. If you and I are so many individuals, here just because our forefathers came here to make money and we got left behind, and we continue to be just so many individuals without the will, the collective will to assert our right to be ourselves, then we must perish.　　　　　　　　　　　　　　　1967

———◇◦◇———

Imagine what would happen if we towed Singapore out and left it in the middle of the South Pacific. Instead of two million active and vigorous Singaporeans, you have South-Sea Islanders with flowers in their hair, dancing to languorous tunes. Also, instead of having the enormous sea and air traffic, and the stimulus of people bringing new ideas, we have South-Sea Islanders lounging on the beach, watching the occasional cargo ship drop anchor. Then we would never have developed what we have: three deep-sea harbours, Tanjong Pagar, with berthing alongside for 30 ships, Sembawang, servicing what was up till very recently one of the greatest navies in the world, the deepwater berth at Jurong, not to mention Telok Ayer Basin, Collyer Quay and Kallang Basin, the earliest harbours in the days of the sailing ships. We would not have four airfields, Paya Lebar, Tengah, Changi and Seletar. Nor a network of roads, probably amongst the best maintained in South Asia, telephones and telecommunications that link us up with one another and with all the major cities of the world, and soon a satellite receiving station. In short, if Singapore were in the South Pacific, populated by South-Sea Islanders and not Singaporeans, it would not be able to feed a population of even 20,000 people. But we are not in the South Pacific, nor are we South-Sea Islanders. We do not put flowers on our ears, either as decorative ornaments or as fads like the flower people in the West.　　　1968

Singapore used to be a conglomeration of migrants, each man for himself. If he cared for anybody else at all, it was his own immediate family. Singaporeans now, particularly those born and educated here, are aware that personal survival is not enough. What we have can be preserved only if we together defend the integrity of our country and secure the interests of the whole community.   1968

—◦—

Singapore's objective is not just industrialisation. The development of the economy is very important. But equally important is the development of the nature of our society. We do not want our workers submissive, docile, toadying up to the foreman, the foreman to the supervisor and the supervisor to the boss for increments and promotions. To survive as a separate and distinct community we have to be a proud and rugged people, or we fail. You can neither be proud nor rugged if you have not got self-respect. Self-respect is what our trade unions have and will give to our workers, that protection for a man's right to his own dignity, his dignity as a human being, as a citizen. He may be an unskilled worker, but he is one of us. He must be prepared to fight and die for Singapore. He will neither be able nor willing to do this if he is a cringing coward.   1969

—◦—

We must continue to show the same cheerful courtesy and friendliness to all visitors. We were already known as a clean, green and thriving city. No amount of tourist promotion can equal the personal verdict of people who have visited us, and found us friendly and courteous, honest and efficient. 1971

—◦—

You know the Singaporean. He is a hard-working, industrious, rugged individual. Or we would not have made the grade. But let us also recognise that he is a champion grumbler.   1977

I am proud of the ethos with which we have infused a younger generation of Singaporeans. We have given them the chance to stand up, be self-reliant, and be enough of a team, of a nation, so that all can perform at their best, and the whole group, including the losers, will not perish. And that is achieved by going with human instincts, going with basic culture, and making adjustments along the way for those who would otherwise lose.   1989

———<○>———

The Singapore worker is not psychologically geared to be as independent-minded and resilient as the Hong Kong worker. The Singapore worker votes for his government and then expects his ministers to take care of his livelihood and his children's future. On the other hand, Hong Kong people are very independent-minded. They expect little of the colonial government. This is the key to understanding Hong Kong's dynamism.   1992

———<○>———

Singaporeans seldom try because they fear failing. One said: 'No risk, no failure' is the Singapore *kiasu* motto. Instead Singapore's motto should be 'Who Dares Wins', that of the British SAS.   1993

———<○>———

An island city-state in Southeast Asia could not be ordinary if it was to survive. We had to make extraordinary efforts to become a tightly knit, rugged and adaptable people who could do things better and cheaper than our neighbours, because they wanted to bypass us and render obsolete our role as the entrepôt and middleman for the trade of the region. We had to be different.   2000

ON COLONIALISM

Colonialism is on the way out but it is not moving fast enough. We, in the People's Action Party, intend to give colonialism a final push and sink it for good in Southeast Asia.

1955

———<><>———

We shall seek to repeal the National Service Ordinance. We are not, in principle, opposed to conscription but we believe that only an independent government freely chosen by the people and responsible to them has the right to ask its citizens to die for it.

1955

———<><>———

The large mass of the people of this country are nationalists. They have learnt to hate a colonial Malaya because it has degraded them and lost them their self-respect. It has not given them a world in which they can live as self-respecting human beings in a peaceful and happy society, where the wealth of the country is developed for the benefit of the people of the country and not for the benefit of those who, for reasons of military might, have taken political control of this territory.

1955

———<><>———

The day I can say, 'I am a free man. This is my country', that day I will welcome you as a friendly host would do a guest. But I will not be a guest in my own country.

1955

It is no use to tell the people: 'You cannot have democracy. You are not fit for it. You will be devoured by the communists. Let us first fight the communists.' It does not work. It does not strike one bell anywhere in the hearts of any patriotic Malayan who would wish to see an independent, democratic, non-communist Malaya. We are not prepared to fight to perpetuate or to prolong the colonial system. But give us our rights and we will fight the communists or any others who threaten the existence of an independent, democratic, non-communist Malaya.

1955

———⊙◦⊃———

We in the People's Action Party believe that freedom is the inalienable right of any people anywhere in the world, and it is not for any retired diplomat who has travelled across Saudi Arabia or any colonial official to say that we are not fit to run; we are not fit to walk; we are not even fit to stand on our own feet.

1955

———⊙◦⊃———

It is not enough just to have efficient routine officers who can write good minutes. It is vital that you find men with imagination, drive, integrity and purpose to make Malaya a thriving socialist democracy. Those who take over the white men's jobs must realise that not only their pensions, and their future prospects of promotion, but the future of a democratic parliamentary State depends upon whether or not they discharge their duties with honour and credit. Unfortunately in the past people have been chosen for the service, not because it was believed that they had signal qualities for service to their fellow men, but because they had the signal qualities of docility and subservience to their white rulers.

1956

Repression is a habit that grows. I am told it is like making love – it is always easier the second time! The first time there may be pangs of conscience, a sense of guilt. But once embarked on this course, with constant repetition, you get more and more brazen in the attack and in the scope of the attack. First, the conscience is disturbed by a sense of guilt. You attack only those whom your Special Branch can definitely say are communists. They have no proof except what X told Z who told Alpha who told Beta who told the Special Branch. Then you attack those whom your Special Branch say are actively sympathising with and helping the communists, although they are not communists themselves. Then you attack those whom your Special Branch say, although they are not communists or fellow travellers, yet, by their intransigent opposition to any collaboration with colonialism, they encourage the spirit of revolt and weaken constituted authority and thereby, according to the Special Branch, they are aiding the communists. Then finally, since you have gone that far, you attack all those who oppose you.   1956

With Merdeka[1] will come greater responsibilities, harder work, a greater sense of purpose and a sense of endeavour. We must resist this tendency that Merdeka means grabbing the white man's job, grabbing the white man's house, grabbing the white man's car and shaking legs like he used to shake legs before. That is not our idea of Merdeka.   1956

With Merdeka, we must see that the country's labour and natural resources will bear more economic fruits than ever before. And we must so order our society that these fruits are distributed for the benefits and enjoyment of all our people, not for any privileged exploiting group be they foreign or local. Then only will Merdeka have its full meaning for all the people of Malaya.

1957

I think the people of Malaya have no regrets in the passing of the British Raj. But I give this one compliment to the British Raj. They, of all the colonial powers, know how to bow out gracefully. Unlike the French and the Dutch who got their brains beaten into the dust of Hanoi and Yogyakarta, the British are past masters at this art. They bow out gracefully when the time comes.

1957

———

The wealth of opportunity which early independence has presented to our youth is something which in later years your children will read like the *Arabian Nights*. You can graduate in 1960, you can become a deputy secretary of a ministry by 1965, you might even become a permanent secretary in 1970.

1960

———

The Portuguese, the Dutch, the British and the French, they came to Southeast Asia and divided it up amongst themselves, much in the fashion of modern gangsters who demarcate their respective territorial jurisdictions over a city. Geography they condemned. And the course of history they distorted. During that colonial era, the links between Jakarta and Amsterdam, between Singapore and London were closer than the links between Jakarta and Singapore. Such were the absurdities of European colonial domination.   1960

———

I speak for one and all of you that we have had enough of being pawns and playthings of foreign powers. We have a will of our own, and a right to live in peace on our own. So let us unite in Malaysia and prevent it ever from happening again. And let us settle these legacies of World War II peacefully if we may, but otherwise if we must.   1963

In the minds of the people of Asia and indeed of Africa, it used to be believed that independence was an automatic solution to all men's ills and that with independence would come prosperity and glory. The need for a sound administration and an economy that ticks was never thought of by anyone other than the few who had to govern. 1963

—◦—

We must resolve to defend ourselves to the death, for death is preferable to conquest and absorption. When our neighbours, both friendly and unfriendly, understand this, then peace in Southeast Asia is more likely to be preserved. Whatever the economic pressures, whatever the harassment by sabotage, whatever the psychological tensions, let no one mistake our right to be masters in our own house. 1963

—◦—

The problem of adjustment is acute for both the coloniser and the colonised. For the former imperial powers, they have to get used to their new circumstances and formulate a new role for themselves in a changed world. For the new countries, they must rid themselves of the illusion that now they can go back to an idyllic past when there was a satisfying society – sometimes of natural socialism – which the white man came and destroyed. Romanticism, however natural, is fatal to progress. What has happened is irreversible, and the choice before each of us is what to make of the future, not how to re-live the past. 1966

—◦—

The remarkable way in which the [British] Empire was dismantled, consciously, and with the minimum of animosity and antipathy, means goodwill. And goodwill, another way of describing trust and confidence as a result of long association, is not without economic value. 1969

My generation was old enough to remember the nightmare of the three and a
half years of Japanese military administration. Inflation, corruption, black-
marketing, the debasement of public and personal life, they were the order
of things. But we were young, and proud enough, to believe that one day we
could, and we would, govern Singapore better than either the Japanese or the
British, if only because we cared and felt more passionately for our people.

1970

—<><>—

The Dutch, the British, the French never gave us any technology. They
built our universities, but they never taught us engineering. They taught
us medicine, law, history, culture. They withheld the modern part of the
industrial society.

1996

27

ON MERGER AND SEPARATION WITH MALAYSIA

Singapore must join the Federation to become an independent nation. We must therefore strive to make merger easier, first by increasing amity and unity between the different races in Malaya. The Malays are in the majority in the Federation. The Chinese in Singapore. Therefore it is imperative to make the Malays in the Federation understand that other races, the Indian and particularly the Chinese are their brothers who want to work and live together for our common happiness and welfare. When we have achieved merger and independence, we can fight through the democratic system of government of one man, one vote in free and secret elections, to establish a socialist society. One man, one vote means in the end that the poor people of Malaya who are in the majority have the constitutional power to elect the majority of the representatives in our Malayan Parliament and therefore the right to govern and change the order of society.

1957

―⊚―

Alone and isolated, no government in Singapore can solve the problems of unemployment and growing economic difficulties which will in its turn bring in social unrest and ultimately chaos. Merged with the Federation, with local autonomy in education and labour policies to suit our special circumstances, we will have a viable economic base, and the essentials of a solution of our problems of an expanding population without an equally expanding economy.

1961

―⊚―

No one disputes that Singapore and the Federation are one. No one disputes that it was the British colonial government that divided these two territories for their own political convenience. We are one country and one people. We must reunite. The only question is when and how.

1961

The first sacred duty to the people was to ensure the permanent security and prosperity of Singapore, which is only possible in a merger with the Federation. Any other way meant isolation, meant playing to the communists.

1962

—◦—

A nation is great not by its size alone. It is the will, the cohesion, the stamina, the discipline of its people and the quality of their leaders which ensure it an honourable place in history. By Asian standards, Malaysia is a small nation. But let no one doubt the will, cohesion, endurance and the discipline of her people, and let no one misjudge the resolve of her leaders.

1963

—◦—

When our survival is at stake, those who help the enemy to weaken the nation will find to their cost that the nation is prepared to defend itself against the enemy without, and also so against the enemy within [...] If ever the communists succeed in weakening our resolve for Malaysia, then verily first Sarawak, then Sabah, then Singapore, and finally Malaya itself will be slowly absorbed into the Indonesian orbit.

1963

—◦—

Countries like individuals have to grow up and face the facts of life. They have to learn how to live with their neighbours and fend for themselves in a harsh and predatory world. For over 300 years, European colonial domination reduced to near-perpetual tutelage large portions of Asia. And so it is, that we in Malaysia until recently did not have to take upon ourselves the harsh burden of finding our place in a turbulent part of the world in which we are not far from being the richest, whilst we are very far from being the strongest.

1963

Malaysia has a future as long as we have faith and confidence in ourselves, and as long as the leaders have confidence in each other's good faith. I give you my word that as long as there are men like the Tunku[2] at the helm and we are in charge in Singapore we can make Malaysia succeed, and succeed it will. Banish all doubts and fears from your minds. The future is always full of challenge and trials. We can and will surmount them.   1964

—◦—

The world did not owe us a living. We did not owe Malaya a living. Neither did they owe us a living. But they either kill themselves trying to crush Singapore, or we kill ourselves trying to undermine them, or we try and make a go of it together with Sabah and Sarawak.   1964

—◦—

Singapore shall be forever a sovereign democratic and independent nation, founded upon the principles of liberty and justice and ever seeking the welfare and happiness of her people in a more just and equal society.[3]   1965

—◦—

Every time we look back on this moment when we signed this agreement which severed Singapore from Malaysia, it will be a moment of anguish. For me it is a moment of anguish because all my life ... you see, the whole of my adult life ... I have believed in Malaysia, merger and the unity of these two territories. You know, it's a people, connected by geography, economics and ties of kinship ... Would you mind if we stop for a while?   1965

—◦—

This is not a Chinese country. Singapore is not a Chinese country nor a Malay country nor an Indian country. That is why we said before that a Malaysian Malaysia is not a Malay country; that was why I was not satisfied.   1965

Although our house is small, in our house, how we arrange the tables and the chairs and the beds is our own affair. Not our friends' or our neighbours' affairs. No one has the right to say that the bed should be moved over there, the chair should be moved over here. This is our house. Although it is small, it is our property. It is the right of the people of Singapore to manage Singapore as the people of Singapore want it to be.   1965

———

I would like to emphasise that so far as we are concerned, we are one people in two countries. All that separation [from Malaysia] has done is to divide the one society into two not altogether dissimilar parts. But whereas before we would have sought one solution for the whole, now there are two experiments being carried out in these two halves. And the experiments on how to find a solution to the problems of multiracialism, multilingualism and a multiplicity of religion, and the policies pursued in any one half are bound to have repercussions on the attitudes and assessments on the other side; and the side which produces a successful solution is the side whose views will ultimately prevail.   1965

———

I would like to believe that the two years we spent in Malaysia are years which will not be easily forgotten, years in which the people of migrant stock here who are a majority learnt of the terrors and the follies and the bitterness which is generated when one group tries to assert its dominance over the other on the basis of one race, one language, one religion. It is because of this that my colleagues and I were determined, as from the moment of separation, that this lesson will never be forgotten. So it is that into the Constitution of the Republic of Singapore will be built safeguards, in so far as the human mind can devise means whereby the conglomeration of numbers, of likeness, as a result of affinities of race or language or culture, shall never work to the detriment of those who, by the accident of history, find themselves in minority groups in Singapore.   1965

We planned that there should be one united Malaya, comprising the peninsula and Singapore. It ended up with one Federation of Malaysia comprising Sarawak and North Borneo, but excluding Singapore. History does not happen in clean-cut units like courses for credits in an American university. It is after forces let loose in tumultuous events have run their course that the historian comes along to mark out neat periods and narrates them in clear-cut chapters. 1980

———

Twenty years ago, I declared Singapore an independent republic. Many let off firecrackers to celebrate our abrupt separation from Malaysia. They felt released from the oppression of communal politics. But I was far from jubilant. I was fearful of the problems of survival. Our old way of making a living as the entrepôt centre for Malaysia was to disappear. How were we to make a living without the hinterland of Malaysia to back us? It has been one ceaseless search for new ways to make ourselves economically relevant to the world. Our assets were our geographic location, our infrastructure in communication and transportation, and a hard-working people. We reached out to the developed world – America, Japan, and Western Europe. We manufactured and exported to them and to the rest of the world. 1985

———

Some countries are born independent. Some achieve independence. Singapore had independence thrust upon it. 1998

———

She [Madame Kwa Geok Choo[4]] had an uncanny ability to read the character of a person. She would sometimes warn me to be careful of certain persons and often she turned out to be right. When we were about to join Malaysia, she told me that we would not succeed because the UMNO Malay leaders had such different lifestyles and because their politics were communally based on race and religion. I replied that we had no choice, and that we had to make it work. But she was right, we were asked to leave Malaysia before two years. 2010

ON THE FUTURE

Singaporeans must be made aware of the dangers lurking ahead in an age of great changes and uncertainties. We take the future for granted only at our own peril. We have survived because we are a practical and a realistic people.

1955

It is not so easy either for the British, the communist or the nationalist to foretell what lies ahead. It is like the song that goes: 'What will I be when I grow up? Will I be handsome, will I be rich?' And the refrain is: 'The future's not ours to see.' If we want to know what is going to happen in the future, we must know what are the forces at work. And having decided our position, we then try and work these forces in our favour.

1956

The future is what we make of it. We owe it to ourselves to give of our best to build the foundations of a harmonious and integrated nation, peaceful, prosperous and vigilant, a haven of tolerance, harmony and progress in the stormy seas of Southeast Asia.

1964

To understand the present and anticipate the future, one must know enough of the past, enough to have a sense of the history of a people. One must appreciate not merely what took place but more especially why it took place and in that particular way. This is true of individuals, as it is for nations. The personal experience of a person determines whether he likes or hates certain things, welcomes them or fears them when they recur. So it is with nations: it is the collective memory of a people, the composite learning from past events which led to successes or disasters that makes a people welcome or fear new events because they recognise parts in new events which have similarities with past experience.   1980

—◦◦—

Singapore's lifestyles and its political vocabulary have been heavily influenced by the West. I assess Western influence at 60 per cent, compared to the influence of core Asian values at 40 per cent. In 20 years, this ratio will shift, as East Asia successfully produces its own mass products and coins its own political vocabulary. The influence of the West on our lifestyles, foods, fashions, politics and the media, will drop to 40 per cent and Asian influence will increase to 60 per cent.   1995

—◦◦—

We are not Australia. Australia will grow wheat, have cattle and sheep, but Singapore is man-made, it services the needs of the international community and if those needs change either because technology has changed or worse, because the political and security set-up is adverse for development in this region, we will shrivel on the vine. You look at Venice. The Ottoman Empire came. The Silk Road became impassable, ships went round the Cape. Venice declined.   1995

The future is as full of promise as it is fraught with uncertainty. The industrial society is giving way to one based on knowledge. The new divide in the world will be between those with the knowledge and those without. We must learn to be part of the knowledge-based world.   2000

Fast forward and imagine China 100 years from now with a 1.8 billion people. It will be at least five, if not ten times, Japan in GDP and with the capabilities in high-tech that the Japanese have. Now ask ourselves: How do we in Singapore find our place in such an outcome? This is the immense challenge that Singapore and indeed all in Southeast Asia face. Our way forward is to upgrade our levels of education, skills, knowledge and technology. Life-long learning is a must for everyone in this knowledge economy with rapidly changing technology.   2001

The energy problem arises out of man's ingenuity and man's innate instinct to proliferate. Whatever he does, he fills up occupied space, that is the end result. From one million Singaporeans in 1940, we now have four million. Is it sustainable? I don't know. I don't think it is sustainable indefinitely.   2003

Friends tell me many young Singaporeans believe Singapore's best years are behind us. Because we made from Third World to First in one generation they believe that there will be no further dramatic transformations in their lifetime, that the best pickings of cheap standalone houses that their elders got are no longer available. They are pessimists and wrong. Singapore is like an aircraft flying at 30,000 ft. We have another 6,000 ft to rise to 36,000 ft, the height top US and EU airlines are flying. Furthermore we have not reached First World standards in the finer things in life, music, culture and the arts, the graces of a civilised society. The generation now in their 30s to 50s can take Singapore there in the next 15 to 20 years. The best is yet to be.   2004

ON THE GREENING
OF SINGAPORE

We shall have more green parks and gardens, swimming pools, recreational facilities like the East Coast Lagoon with its chalets and picnic areas, the beaches of the Southern Islands and the holiday camps at St. John's Island. Few cities in Asia have such recreational outlets for their people.　　1976

—⊶—

Even in the sixties, when the government had to grapple with grave problems of unemployment, lack of housing, health and education, I pushed for the planting of trees and shrubs. I have always believed that a blighted urban jungle of concrete destroys the human spirit. We need the greenery of nature to lift up our spirits. So in 1967, I launched the Garden City programme to green up the whole island and try to make it into a garden.　　1995

—⊶—

Without the greening effort, Singapore would have been a barren, ugly city. There would have been few trees, planted haphazardly here and there, but there would have been none of the planning or the care and maintenance that sustain our greenery today.　　2012

—⊶—

We used to have tree-planting days when thousands were mobilised. But as the whole place is greened up now, you have to find a way to get students to realise what it takes to grow these trees and plants. The present group of leaders must think of ways and means to get the younger generation to buy into the greening of Singapore, to take ownership of it.　　2012

ON ARTS AND HERITAGE

The past is important. It enables us to better understand the future. It reinforces our determination to overcome our problems, to build a more secure, a more rewarding future for our children.

1970

———◦———

These great [Chinese] rituals are important. The festivals and rituals remind us of our past and identify ourselves with the history of our ancestors. Our history did not begin when our forefathers came to Singapore. It goes back deep into the beginnings of Chinese civilisation over 5,000 years ago. That history is a part of us because of the tradition and culture they have bequeathed us.

1991

———◦———

We made our share of mistakes in Singapore. For example in our rush to rebuild Singapore, we knocked down many old and quaint Singapore buildings. Then we realised we were destroying a valuable part of our cultural heritage, that we were demolishing what tourists found attractive and unique in Singapore. We halted the demolition. Instead we undertook extensive conservation and restoration of ethnic districts such as Chinatown, Little India and Kampong Glam and of the civic district, with its colonial era buildings [...] The value of these areas in architectural, cultural and tourism terms cannot be quantified only in dollars and cents.

1995

———◦———

As a nation, we must have other goals. Economic growth is not the end itself. After the success of the economy, you want to translate it into high standards of living, high quality of life, with recreation, the arts, spiritual fulfilment, and intellectual fulfilment. So, we are also spending considerable sums for the arts, which will create a more gracious society.

1995

For the benefit of the younger generation, the Chinese clans should build up their archival records and make them easily accessible. The rich experience and recollections of older Singaporeans should be carefully chronicled. It will be a pity if their knowledge of the past is lost in this information age. The Chinese clans should make good use of IT to store records of historical significance. They can use multimedia technology to present history in an interesting and lively way. 1997

The old model on which I worked was to create a First World city in a Third World region – clean, green, efficient, a pleasant, healthy and wholesome society, safe and secure for everyone. These virtues are no longer sufficient. Now we have also to be an economically vibrant and an exciting city to visit, with top-class symphony orchestras, concerts, drama, plays, artists and singers and popular entertainment. These are the lifestyles international professionals and executives seek. 2005

Heritage is not something static, lying hidden to be discovered, admired and conserved. It is a part of the lives of a people, and it shapes the ways a people meet new challenges and helps them adapt to survive. 2005

We used to be derided as just clean, green, safe and orderly, but dull and antiseptic. Now we have a lively city with the arts, culture, museums, art galleries, the Esplanade Theatre by the Bay, a Western orchestra, a Chinese orchestra. Musical groups perform for the public outside the Esplanade Theatre. And we have resident writers and artists. 2010

ON POLITICS

Politics is about human beings and their lives. It is an art, not a science. It is the art of the possible. In Singapore, it means what is possible, given a hardworking people, with a realistic understanding of our narrow economic base and the need for social discipline and high performance, to keep ahead of other developing countries with low wages and more natural resources.   1955

The real action is in the constituency. My first lesson in politics was that the speeches made in Parliament did not count as much as the speeches I made [during] *fang wen* [visits] on constituency tours.   1955

Those without this indomitable fighting spirit had better go and sell stocks and shares. This task [politics] is not for the faint-hearted. It is for people with deep and abiding convictions.   1955

Some people believe that, having debauched themselves in one political party or front, they can, like the phoenix, arise from the ashes of the old in the feathers of a new party, front or movement as fresh as if nothing had happened. In fact, there is no such magic formula for longevity in political life other than the simple and the obvious: just honour your promises; do not corrupt and debauch your party.   1956

In the heat of election battle, people and political parties tend to be sidetracked onto minor and irrelevant issues. In Singapore, as you know, the habit is to do two things. First insult and denigrate your opponents. Second, promise the electorate anything and everything – the sun, the moon and the stars. You [the voters] have had your fill of this and you must be pretty fed up with it. And quite rightly so.   1957

———◦◦———

It is the business of every government to see that it governs in such a way that it is returned to power at the end of its mandate, and the fact is that there is nothing improper in this purpose. It is the whole business of a government to govern in such a way that at the end of its term of office, the people say, 'Yes, we shall have more of it. We entrust our fate to you for another term of office.'   1957

———◦◦———

The theory of the democratic state is that there is a good motor car in good mechanical condition, with mechanics, fitters and so on to keep it sound. And there is a driver there to take the minister where he wants to go. It is for the minister, having been elected by the people, to decide where the driver is to go and how and by what route. It is the business of the civil service – the driver, the fitters and the rest – to keep that car in sound mechanical condition.   1957

———◦◦———

For reasons which I thought to be in the interests of the people, I did not attend a particular meeting in Kuala Lumpur and chose to stay in the Cameron Highlands with the Prime Minister of the Federation who was golfing with me. Golf is a very necessary asset in Malaysia, and a lot of valuable and important information was imparted and analysed in the leisurely and sometimes enlightened and rarified atmosphere of the highlands. On many an occasion I thought perhaps if only members on the other side played golf, they would not have made some of the colossal blunders that they had.   1963

It is in our postures that we give an indication of whether we are growing up to the realities of life in Southeast Asia or whether we are still adolescents in a world of make-believe, of sheriffs and bandits, of revolutionary anti-colonialists and wicked white colonial exploiters.   1964

—◦◦—

There are very few fundamentally new moves by colonialists, communists or communalists which we have not in turn encountered and checkmated in the past. Every ploy, each feint, every distraction, either for internal or international consumption, we have watched, studied, parried and been ready to counter the real blow which was to be delivered.   1967

—◦◦—

If democratic socialists are to make a contribution to the course of events, they must cease to think in terms of abstractions. They must give meaning to socialist ideals in pragmatic and realistic policies to produce changes for the better in the daily lives of their peoples.   1967

—◦◦—

[Politics] is a marathon, not a hundred yards spurt. With every passing speech, with every passing act, the character, the style, the strength, the weaknesses are etched in the minds of the public. You can do a PR job, as has been written in American books after the making of presidents, where you have a vast electorate of 200 million people with over 120 million potential voters with the help of radio and TV, and you suddenly find with a whole host of ghostwriters and advisers, that the man becomes scholarly, learned, solicitous in his speech. Catch him at a press conference and a question-and-answer session, where the ghosts cannot whisper to him, and the man is betrayed.   1977

If you want to be popular, do not try to be popular all the time. Popular government does not mean that you do popular things all the time. We do not want to be unpopular or to do unpopular things. But when they are necessary, they will be done. 1977

It is no longer in the interest of Singapore for the 1980s that the old guards should exert their dominance to exclude the Opposition in a general election so that distraction from our vital goals is minimised. We did this for the 1960s and '70s in order that the people could concentrate on the urgent tasks of survival. The position has changed, not just the challenges confronting us but also the nature of the electorate. 1984

From our perilous years in the '50s and '60s, a whole generation of Singaporeans was educated in a harsh political school. They were wise to the ways of an irresponsible Opposition and did not vote for any in four successive general elections. [...] They need no further lessons. Nor do the older ministers. But my generation has grown 25 years older. Our children have no memories of troubled times from reckless Opposition. A younger generation of ministers also missed this experience. Fierce combat has made the older ministers what they are. For those amongst us, the older ones that were weak or slow or nervous, they became early casualties. Those present are survivors of a Darwinian process of natural selection. We have keen survial instincts, familiar with every trick, underhand or dastardly manoeuvre. We know how to deal with every scoundrel. 1984

An MP must now not only be good at speaking but also at getting things done. When an estate is dirty, lifts out of order, and rubbish not regularly and properly collected, that is when residents realise that without regular maintenance, the value of their flats will drop. 1992

In one of my talks to the university students before I stepped down, I quoted Theodore Roosevelt who in 1901 said: 'Talk softly, but carry a big stick.' Every PM has to have a big stick. If he doesn't want to carry the big stick, then he has got to have somebody carry it for him.   1995

———◦———

How do you think today's Singapore came about? Because everyone knows if I say that we are going in a certain direction and that we're going to achieve this objective, if you set out to block me, I will take a bulldozer and clear the obstruction. I leave nobody in any doubt that is where we are going and that any obstruction will be cleared. So there were very few obstructions. So we got the highway cleared and travelled to our destination.   1995

———◦———

However good the government, there will always be voters who are disappointed and dissatisfied with the government, and who want to have opposition MPs. But no opposition party has been able to assemble a team which is a credible alternative government. The reason, I believe, is that our talent pool is small. And over the last 30 years the PAP has been methodical and diligent in scouring for talent, to persuade, cajole and conscript the best into public life.   1996

———◦———

I cannot envisage an alternative government emerging through political dissidents and oppositionists coming together to produce an alternative programme. There just is no viable alternative programme for an island city state other than what we have empirically worked out in the last 30 years. This is why the able and talented have not come forward to form a credible alternative team and challenge the PAP. They know the PAP is doing the right thing, and there is no alternative way. They are content to thrive and prosper with the present men in charge. Those who have come forward to be an alternative to the PAP are mostly lightweights or, worse, flawed characters.
1996

We must always remember we are not an ordinary country like Australia, or New Zealand, or Canada, or Britain, or the USA. There people can vote for one party or another, and life will go on. If we do that, the Singapore miracle will come to an end. Put the SDP [Singapore Democratic Party] and/or the WP [Workers' Party] into government and you will see Singapore become like Cinderella and her coach when midnight comes – the coach will turn back into a pumpkin. There is no other party who can run Singapore the way it is run.   1996

—◦○◦—

When you put up an idea which I know is wrong and believe profoundly to be wrong and will do us harm, I must crush it. I don't crush you, I crush your idea. I mean, if I'm wrong then my ideas deserve to be crushed. Maybe 'crush' is a harsh word, but this is a harsh world. It is a contest of whose idea is right because if it is wrong, we are going to do harm to many people.   1996

—◦○◦—

There is no level playing field of any government helping its opposition to win votes.   2006

—◦○◦—

You assume that politics is about elections and election contests. I do not see politics that way. If you look it up in a dictionary, I think the best definition of politics is what I found in an American dictionary which said 'the art or science of governance of a country and how it runs its internal and external relations'. Now, that's a very abstract concept. Translated in real life it means: 'How is my life affected by the government? Do I have a job? Do I have a home? Do I have medicine when I need it? Do I have enough recreational facilities? Is there a future for my children? Will they be educated? Will there be a chance to advance yourself?   2006

ON DEMOCRACY

It [an identity card system] is a marked departure from the normal traditions of a liberal civilised society [...] It is part of the regimentation of a police state, and one of the things we accuse the communists of doing, that they document people; they regiment them; they get everybody docketed in dossiers. We, in a liberal democracy, believe in liberal conditions. We value human freedom and the liberty of the individual.

1955

If you believe in democracy, you must believe in it unconditionally. If you believe that men should be free, then they should have the right of free association, of free speech, of free publication.

1955

Let me reduce to its barest essentials what we on this side of the House believe to be the democratic system. It means a system where each man has as much a right to live in this world as the next man, and where it is possible for the majority of the people to bring about changes in the social order without resorting to force. Translated into political terms, it means giving one man, one vote, and allowing him to decide who should govern, and how they should govern for a specified number of years. It means the right at the end of that specified number of years again to pass judgment on that government and on others who may present themselves for the mandate of the people.

1957

Of course, there are some people you must protect from their own gullibility.

1962

The fact that you have got a few activists going to the same meetings and working up steam, doesn't mean you've got votes. It's when you open the ballot boxes that you know whether the steam that you have generated has warmed anybody's heart.   1976

From my experience, constitutions have to be custom-made, tailored to suit the peculiarities of the person wearing the suit. Perhaps, like shoes, the older they are, the better they fit. Stretch them, soften them, resole them, repair them. They are always better than a brand new pair of shoes. Our people have got used to and understand the present system. It takes a long time – like discarding dialects and learning Mandarin. Any fundamental change takes a long time. But most important of all, the Constitution works. Many countries have tried and gone through several constitutions since independence, from prime minister and parliamentary systems to presidential government, on to military rule, back to elections for a president, on to a people's republic, back to a revolutionary junta. They have not brought stability or legitimacy. I believe it is better to stretch and ease an old shoe when we know that the different shape and fit of a younger generation requires a change. It is a change to meet the future.   1984

One man, one vote is a most difficult form of government. From time to time the results can be erratic. People are sometimes fickle. They get bored with stable, steady improvements in life, and in a reckless moment they vote for a change for change's sake.   1984

In new countries, democracy has worked and produced results only when there is an honest and effective government, which means a people smart enough to elect such a government. Remember, elected governments are only as good as the people who choose them.   1988

One great advantage my government enjoyed in Singapore was the support of the people for the difficult policies we had to implement [...] The people gave my government solid support and cooperation freely expressed by secret ballot in multiparty general elections held every 4 to 5 years.

1991

———◇———

Is democracy universally valid? After World War II when the British and French dismantled their empires in the 1940s–60s, the British and French governments gave their newly independent colonies democratic constitutions modelled on their own. There were over 40 British-type and over 25 French-type constitutions. Twenty to forty years since then, the results have been patchy and uneven. In spite of this, the West led by America puts the credo simply as 'democracy is universally good for all peoples', and that to progress, modernise and become industrial societies, they should become democracies.

1991

———◇———

The weakness of democracy is that the assumption that all men are equal and capable of equal contribution to the common good is flawed.

1992

———◇———

Contrary to what American political commentators say, I do not believe that democracy necessarily leads to development. I believe that what a country needs to develop is discipline more than democracy. The exuberance of democracy leads to undisciplined and disorderly conditions which are inimical to development. The ultimate test of the value of a political system is whether it helps that society to establish conditions which improve the standard of living for the majority of its people plus enabling the maximum of personal freedoms compatible with the freedoms of others in society.

1992

All peoples of all countries need good government. A country must first have economic development, then democracy may follow. With a few exceptions, democracy has not brought good government to new developing countries.

1992

———◇———

There are some flaws in the assumptions made for democracy. It is assumed that all men and women are equal or should be equal. Hence, one man, one vote. But is equality realistic? If it is not, to insist on equality must lead to regression. Let me put it to the test in some theoretical situations. If we had a world government for this small interdependent world, will one man, one vote lead to progress or regression? All can immediately see that the developed and educated peoples of the world will be swamped by the undeveloped and the uneducated, and that no progress will be possible.   1992

———◇———

Jeyaretnam[5] says he has drawn Cheng San out of a hat and that an election win will be a birthday present for him. It will be a very expensive birthday present for the people of Cheng San.

1996

———◇———

The problem now is how to work the system of one man, one vote when we have to get quality leadership to the top. If we leave it to natural processes it will be a contest on television performances as in the West. And the best television performers and rally entertainers are not necessarily the best leaders who can deliver good government.

1996

———◇———

We cannot afford to forget that public order, personal security, economic and social progress and prosperity are not the natural order of things, that they depend on ceaseless effort and attention from honest and effective government that the people must elect.

2000

One weakness of the democratic system is that voters do not have a proper assessment of the real person behind a first-time candidate – his character, steadfastness, trustworthiness. The voters know their candidate only after several years. This is true of ministers, the Speaker, of every MP including Opposition MPs [...] Hence it is important that MPs be suitably remunerated. People need time to gauge and assess who has what qualities and is best suited for what jobs that can make Singapore grow and thrive. The danger for Singapore is a sudden change, a new school term with new pupils, new prefects, new head prefect, and new principal. Things will go awry. Hence the importance of continuity.

2000

—⊸∘⊶—

A free and fair election is not the best first step to nurture a democracy in a country that has no history or tradition of self-government. Without adequate preparations elections will allow a people to vent their frustrations against the corruption and inadequacies of the incumbents and vote in the opposition. That led to Hamas gaining power in Palestine. A better start would be to educate their young, especially their women, and give them equal job opportunities.

2006

—⊸∘⊶—

There are some who yearn for multiparty politics and rotating party governments. They should study Taiwan, Thailand and the Philippines. Rotating party governments have led to more corruption and misgovernment. And a 'freewheeling press' has not cleaned up corruption, although according to American 'democracy' theories it is designed to do so. Furthermore frequent chop and change in governments and policies have hampered Taiwan's and Thailand's economic growth and increased unemployment and caused political instability.

2008

ON THE PAP

The PAP is an honest and clean party. We are not afraid to tell you as we have done over the years that we believe in a socialist society. That, in this colonial society, we represent the interests of the people of Singapore against the European colonial officials, and vested interests. That we represent the interest of the poor against the rich.　　　　　　　　　　　1955

—◦—

Do not try and out-PAP the PAP. It is a very foolish and unprofitable business.　　　　　　　　　　　1956

—◦—

In our ultimate objectives, the creation of a socialist society, the PAP does not differ from the Malayan Communist Party. But we differ from the communists in methods. We believe in peaceful constitutional methods. We do not believe in the dictatorship of any party or group.　　　　1957

—◦—

The PAP is a party of the people. We view the city council and its magnificent building from the standpoint of the man who stands in the queue at the beginning of each month to pay his bills. And it is to make life less unjust and more comfortable for the man in the queue that the PAP exists.　　　1957

—◦—

My party may have a lot of faults, but there is one fault that it has not got – too much money. We have not got the money to use, but we have drive, talent and the ability to organise.　　　　　　　　　　　1957

We the PAP would prefer to lose an election rather than to win it on false premises and false promises. We have grown from strength to strength because we are honest, because what we say publicly we honour publicly. 1958

———<∘>———

If I were asked to sum up in one sentence what I think was the strongest single feature of the PAP government in the past year, I would say that there was a government prepared to govern firmly, fairly and justly, within the limits of its power, in the interests of the people.   1960

———<∘>———

Every one of you must know that never in the history of Singapore has there been a government more sympathetic, more actively sincere in trying to better the working class.   1961

———<∘>———

The PAP, which was not amenable to manipulation by the British, is not going to be manipulated by the communists.   1961

———<∘>———

In a future full of uncertainties, one factor is certain. The PAP does not run away from problems. We solve them for you and with you. We analyse our difficulties, explain them and propose practical solutions. Then, together, we set out to resolve them.   1976

———<∘>———

Singapore does not have a king or sultan. Nor do we have established political parties which alternate in power. All Singapore has is the PAP.   1990

For 16 years, from 1965 till 1981, we reshaped the political landscape of Singapore. We never abused the people's trust in us, always maintaining rigorous standards of propriety and honesty, and won four successive general elections – 1968, 1972, 1976, 1980 – in clean sweeps. There was no exciting drama, no crowd in the Strangers' Gallery[6]. We made great strides in consolidating our young nation. The only occasion the Strangers' Gallery was full would be the ceremonial openings when the President addressed us. This is a simple litmus test. When the government was in jeopardy, the crowd and pressmen smelling blood, would come to watch the kill, the government being booted out.   1999

—◦◦—

The PAP would be foolish if it refuses or fails to include on its side able and dedicated men of strong political convictions, whether because of differences of personality or unwillingness to adjust policies, and drives them to the Opposition benches. A few sincere and capable leaders could be the spearhead of a group of men and women, able in one or two election terms to present the voters with a shadow cabinet, an alternative team that can match the PAP's. I was able to build up a credible team in one election term, four years after getting elected into this chamber in 1955, because I had talented colleagues to help me plan and implement our strategy outside this chamber. If such a turn of events were to happen, where the PAP is displaced by a leaner, keener and shrewder team, I would not shed any tears over its ouster. For this would be one way to renew the political leadership of Singapore. What would be cause for despair would be if a transient mood of disappointment among the people for some setback or mishap just before an election were to lead them to reject the PAP and vote in a motley crew of incompetents and adventurers. That could end up in tragedy for Singapore. Hence it is important to expose opportunists and incompetents before they can pass themselves off as possible replacements for the PAP.   1999

Will this House see the return of an Opposition that can pose a serious challenge to the PAP? That depends on whether the governing party allows itself to go soft and flabby, ceases to respond creatively to changing circumstances, and so loses its standing with the people.   1999

—◦—

My colleagues and I are sane, rational people even in our moments of anguish. We weigh all possible consequences before we make any move on the political chessboard [...] Our people have the will to fight and the stuff that makes for survival.   2000

—◦—

The very fact that we are not challenged is a pretty strong mandate.   2006

—◦—

There is no easy way to win power or stay in power. If the PAP does not renew itself regularly with fresh blood from the younger generation, stay honest and clean, upgrade the economy and improve the education and skills of our people, to have economic growth and bring a better life to people, it will soon begin to lose seats and eventually be defeated and ousted. So the PAP accepts the realities that the world is changing and we have to adapt ourselves to this different world. We are not stuck in any policy, theory or ideology.   2006

ON LEADERSHIP

I do not yet know of a man who became a leader as a result of having undergone a leadership course. 1957

—◦—

Just honour your promises, do not corrupt and debauch your party and you will find that the people believe you, when you go back to ask them to renew the mandate. 1958

—◦—

I am the captain of the team. Whether we score a resounding success does not depend on the captain alone. Each member of the team has a decisive role to play. And no team ever wins without good teamwork. 1959

—◦—

A good government is expected not only to carry on and maintain standards. It is expected to raise them. 1960

—◦—

The acid test is in performance, not promises. The millions of dispossessed in Asia care not and know not of theory. They want a better life. They want a more equal, a more just society. He who gives them this is their saviour. 1964

The system that we inherited from the British was lopsided. Too much emphasis was laid on the examination and the paper qualification. We were, therefore, rearing a whole generation of softies, who are clever; who wore spectacles but who were weak from want of enough exercise, enough sunshine, and with not enough guts in them. That was all right for a British colony, because the officers came from England [and] had the necessary brawn and toughness. It was they who gave the orders and our people just executed them. That is not good enough. We have to give our own people the orders. And you have to throw up a whole generation capable of that leadership, conscious of its responsibilities, jealous of its rights, not allowing anyone to bully it and push it around, prepared to stand up and fight and die. That kind of a generation will endure till the end of time. 1966

———◦◦———

The deepest compliment we could pay ourselves is to remember that there must come a time – and not so very long – when the torch must be passed on. And there is no greater compliment that a man can pay to himself and to his group than to pass the torch on to like-minded people, fired by the same ideals, but younger, more vigorous, more capable to meet a more contemporary situation. 1967

———◦◦———

One of the reasons why Singapore thrived was because so many of the merchants, both British and non-British, when they gave their word, they kept to it, and the government when it gave its undertaking, invariably honoured it. 1967

Government does not consist only of making speeches. Of course, we need communication and rapport between a people and their leaders. More important are good judgement and bold planning. But most important of all is the confidence, the trust between a people and their government. It is when a people are behind their government, and not at odds with it, that the best results are achieved. When everything looks simple and easy, it means either the gods are on our side, or that the decisions we have made were right.   1969

—◦—

It is not from weakness that one commands respect.   1971

—◦—

If you are impulsive and lucky, you may even pass off as an incisive mind and a decisive commander. If you are unlucky, then you are a hasty bungler and a fool. Or if you take much time for a careful weighing of the odds, but the decision nevertheless turned out wrong, people may well think you are a ditherer, perhaps, even past your prime, and getting on in years, lacking in that ability to be seized of a problem with promptness, and having weighed up the pros and cons, to act decisively. The moral is that if all turns out well, and a decision proves correct, even though taken for the wrong reasons, keep quiet about it. Your judgement may be the better respected.   1973

—◦—

Those hectic years of 1961 till 1963 when every day was a crisis, every morning was a barrage of blows, defections, riots, strikes, arson – vicious, venomous attacks: that's when you know who's got what it takes to be a leader.   1980

From 23 years of experience in government, I have learned that one
high-calibre mind in charge of a ministry, or a statutory board, makes the
difference between success and failure of a major project. A top mind, given
a task, brings together a group of other able men, organises them into a
cohesive team, and away the project goes.

1982

There is a heavy price to pay if mediocrities and opportunists ever take
control of the government of Singapore. And mediocrities and opportunists
can accidentally take over if Singaporeans, in a fit of pique or a moment of
madness, voted for the politics of opposition for the sake of opposition. Five
years of such a government, probably a coalition, and Singapore will be down
on her knees. What has taken decades to build up in social organisation, in
industry, banking, commerce, tourism, will be dismantled and demolished
in a few years. The World Bank has a queue of such broken-back countries
waiting to be mended: Jamaica, Uganda, Ghana, Nicaragua, to name a few
recent casualties seeking emergency World Bank aid. At least they have land
for plantations or mines to dig from, or rivers to be dammed for hydropower
and irrigation. Singapore has only got its strategic location and the people
who can maximize this location by organisation, management, skills and,
most important of all, brains. Once in disarray, it will not be possible to put it
together again.

1982

No resounding ghostwritten speech can ever have the ring of conviction and
sincerity of the words from a Minister who has felt his own problems deeply
and thought them through to their solutions. In several established countries,
average leaders have managed to get by with superb staff back-up. But each
time they go to summit meetings to encounter strong and able leaders of
other nations, their inadequacies show up, painfully and alarmingly.

1982

Great leaders mirror the qualities of the nations they lead. 1985

—◦—

We have continually to draw out younger leaders to fulfil the roles played
by the traditional community leaders. Those with the higher social
conscience must come forward to give of their time to get things done for the
community. This is one of the strengths of Singaporean society, the absence
of class divisions. It grew from our immigrant history. All started at or near
the bottom. The successful immigrants have a tradition of helping the less
successful. 1986

—◦—

Political leaders are judged first, by how effectively they have exercised
their authority in the interests of their people; second, by the way they have
provided for continuity so that a successor government will continue to
protect and advance the interests of their people; third, by the grace with
which they leave office and hand over to their successors. 1988

—◦—

A good administration is essential but in a developing country, let me add, a
good political leadership is critical. It is life and death. In a developed society,
you can have mediocre, indifferent ministers and the country will get by. 1989

—◦—

In a developing country situation, you need a leader of a ministry or a
department who not only understands the ordinary arguments for or against,
but at the end of it says, 'Look, will this work, given our circumstances? Never
mind what the British, what the Australians, what the New Zealanders do.
This is Singapore. Will it work in this situation?' And it is the leader with the
political touch, with the rough and tumble of people, who has to decide. 1989

Good governance includes the pursuit of national interest regardless of theories or ideologies. Good government is pragmatic government.   1993

———⟨∘⟩———

As long as the leaders take care of their people, they will obey the leaders.

1994

———⟨∘⟩———

I have stepped down […] this is my fifth year. I am satisfied with what has happened. Because a government is in place, without me in charge and it is functioning well. I am not without any influence. I attend cabinet meetings and meet the Ministers. And I express my views. But it is the Prime Minister's decisions taken in conjunction with the Ministers. It is a source of pride and satisfaction that I did not leave Singapore without good government.   1995

———⟨∘⟩———

I have collected a group of graduates with a sense of mission, a sense of social purpose, and tried to graft them into the unions so that they can represent union interests. If you want every union leader to spring up from the grassroots, to start off as a blue-collar worker, you will have very uneducated leadership which will be very bad for the unions.   1995

———⟨∘⟩———

For me, they [the major personalities of the 20th century] are Churchill, de Gaulle, Mao, Deng. They changed the world. They were giants, with great ideas. I would hesitate to name Roosevelt because he let himself be dominated by Stalin who was not a great man, who did harm, who incarnated evil, even though he built a strong Soviet Union (that Gorbachev dismantled). The world would have been a better place if Churchill had been able to balance Stalin's influence.   1996

A political leader must be able to persuade people to accept and help push a painful policy which he had decided was necessary and good for the country.

1996

—◦—

Amazingly, throughout most of the contemporary Western world leaders in government require no special training or qualification. Many get elected because they sound and look good on television. The results have been unhappy for their voters.

1996

—◦—

No army, however brave, can win when its generals are weak.

1998

—◦—

Good government of Singapore did not happen naturally. It needed a thorough and meticulous process of selection and testing. Finally, I learnt how the big MNCs [multinational corporations] in America did it, using psychologists and psychiatrists to recruit and to test candidates before promotion. With the help of psychologists and psychiatrists we became better at assessing character and ability. We have assembled together the best persons available and willing. There is no alternative team or group of people outside the government, who can replace the present team.

2000

—◦—

When we started in 1959, my first cabinet of 10, there were only two of us who were born and bred in Singapore. The other eight were born and bred in Malaya, in Ceylon, in South China and abroad. So it was a big catchment from whence the talent came. If we now confine ourselves and in politics we have to confine ourselves to Singapore citizens, I am choosing or I have chosen Ministers who now come from a small talent pool of Singaporeans. If you go to the South China Sea, you're going to catch big tuna, you go to Sentosa Lagoon, you think you're going to get many big tunas?

2003

ON CORRUPTION

If the power of the State which we now control is used not to enrich the lives of many of its people but to line the pockets of a few of the ruling hierarchy, then verily we shall all perish.

1957

———

We don't have to be lawyers to understand right, wrong, good, evil. This is basic and fundamental in the values of a people.

1967

———

Singapore's progress, its verve, its vitality is assured because the administrative machine works. There is no grit. You don't have to grease somebody to crank up the machine. We must keep it that way. To ensure this, I am thinking of an amendment to the law. The innovation is: if any official is found with wealth which cannot be explained and there is uncorroborative evidence of corruption, his whole property can be sequestered.

1967

———

It is sad to see how in many countries, national heroes have let their country slide down the drain to filth and squalor, corruption and degradation, where the kickback and the rake-off has become a way of life, and the whole country sinks in self-debasement and despair. If the political leadership ever allows Singapore to degenerate into these conditions, then we shall perish. For we have not got that agricultural base where you can scatter seed on the ground, and the soil, the rain and the sun will produce you the rice, the corn and the fruits with which to feed yourselves.

1968

Too great a disparity between ministerial rewards and what Ministers, with business experience and professional qualifications, could earn outside will make it increasingly difficult to assemble a successor government. No salary, however generous, can ensure the complete honesty and integrity with which Ministers must discharge their duties. Honest mistakes or errors of judgement by Ministers, however costly, are not as damaging to a country as the suspicion of bias because of corruption. Once a government is tainted with this, the contamination spreads throughout the administration. Then we shall go down the slippery slope, at the bottom of which are carcasses of so many corrupt governments whose peoples have had to suffer for the dishonesty and greed of those in authority.   1973

———◦○◦———

If government workers are adequately paid, they deserved to be punished with severe penalties when they take bribes.   1992

———◦○◦———

The laws against corruption should be tightened to shift the onus of proof onto the person who possesses more assets than his income warrants. Two or three big fish brought to justice successfully, will have a salutary effect on everyone.   1992

———◦○◦———

Once a political system has been corrupted right from the very top leaders to the lowest rungs of the bureaucracy, the problem is very complicated. The cleansing and disinfecting has to start from top and go downwards in a thorough and systematic way. It is a long and laborious process that can be carried out only by a very strong group of leaders with the strength and moral authority derived from unquestioned integrity.   1993

Corruption eats into any system, regardless of the philosophy or ideology of the founding father, of the government, or the location of a country. Even the Communist Party of China and Communist Party of Vietnam, although fired by high ideals, and determined to clean out the corruption and decadence of existing regimes, have become riddled with corruption after a few decades in power. When they abandoned their Marxist ideology and central planning, liberalised their economy to encourage the free market, the percentage, the grease, the kickback, baksheesh returned in great force.   2005

It is a constant fight to keep the house clean. As long as the core leadership is clean, any back sliding can be brought under control and the house cleaned up. What the PAP government cannot ensure is that if it loses an election, a non-PAP government will remain honest. Therefore we have installed constitutional safeguards to meet such an eventuality. We amended the Constitution to have the President popularly elected not by Parliament but by the whole electorate and [he] has a veto power on the spending of the country's reserves by the Cabinet. The President now also has the power to overrule any Prime Minister who stops or holds up an investigation for corruption against any of his Ministers or senior officials or himself.   2005

Money politics is at the heart of the problems in many countries in Asia. 'Money politics' is a codeword for buying of votes to gain power and after gaining power to recover your expenses plus some profit for the next round of vote buying. There is no money politics in Singapore. The integrity of Ministers and public officials is fundamental for political stability. Politics in Singapore is all above board and so has not been troubled by such politicking.

2008

ON HIS CRITICS

The first hallmark of a democratic state, if we are to run a democratic state in Malaya, is tolerance of criticism from other political parties.　　　　　1956

It is very difficult to take seriously opponents who cannot stand up to your punches. One gets a feeling of being cruel to people who, when you knock them down once, stay down for an indefinite length of time.　　　　1957

We all expect lively debates. In fact, it is part of the play of intellect and wit; or if wit is lacking, then at least some buffoonery to take away the tedium and monotony of the day. But one thing I say: in any wicked and deliberate lies, falsehoods and distortions, people play them with their gloves on, but we play them with our gloves off. In this Chamber [Parliament of Singapore] it is bad to expose knuckledusters, but one can use knuckledusters all the same, and outside this Chamber we can well look after ourselves.　　　　1960

I would publicly like to disavow any support from any European or expatriate quarter for the government. I say this unashamedly: that those who wish us well and are non-citizens do best by keeping quiet and praying silently that the country will go on peacefully and prosperously. Those who are against the government and open their big mouths may find a lot of unpleasant consequences.　　　　1961

Not all who oppose the PAP are communists; some are communists, some reactionaries, some opportunists and some merely confused.　　　　1961

We should do well to always remember that if they, the Barisan Sosialis, were in charge of the country, it is very unlikely that we would be allowed, in the Opposition, to say the things of them that we have allowed them to say of us. It is also unlikely in that situation that either in the unions or in the civic organisations we would be allowed even a one-hundredth part of the opportunity that we are now giving them to organise and preach their gospel against the nation. Our failing, I fear, is not that we have stifled democratic rights and liberties, but that we have been too tolerant with a group of men who interpret tolerance as a weakness to be exploited and abused.   1963

My colleagues and I have been accused of arrogance, ineptitude, stupidities. Whatever our faults, we leave the country at the end of our first term of office in a healthier state than we came into office. The last days of the last government were a pathetic sight [...] Morale had collapsed. It was a government that was only interested in its own survival.   1963

Men who have not got the courage to pursue their allegations publicly should desist from making sly and oblique references.   1963

I am not interested in advice from Asian émigrés on what should be in Singapore. Their advice is worse than useless. They have no sense of shame, or they would stay and help their own countries progress and their fellow countrymen live less wretched lives. Instead, they flee to greener pastures and give us advice.   1971

Why should we deliberately ensure that Parliament, henceforth, should have at least a few Opposition Members? There are several reasons. First, from our experience, since December 1981 when the Member for Anson [Jeyaretnam] entered this Chamber, we discovered that there are considerable benefits for younger Ministers and MPs. They have not faced the fearsome foes of the 1950s and '60s. Initially, they were awkward in tackling the Opposition Member. But they soon sharpened their debating skills and they have learned to put down the inanities of the Member for Anson.   1984

—◦—

My colleagues are not intimidated by me. Far from it. They speak their minds. Nothing has happened to them. But if we allow vicious, evil attacks to pass unchallenged – then the whole system must be undermined.   1988

—◦—

The four Opposition MPs have it in their power to lower service and conservancy charges. If they believe in what they said during elections, that PAP means people 'Pay and Pay', now is the time for the four MPs to show they are different and can spend and spend. Let us see if they do what they criticised the PAP for doing. Let us watch whether maintenance standards rise or fall.   1992

—◦—

Everybody now knows that if you take on the PM [Goh Chok Tong], he will have to take you on. That's a plus. I was glad he reacted. If he didn't then more people will throw darts, put a little poison on the tip and throw them at him. And he'll have darts sticking all over him. Supposing I had been a different person and when people throw darts at me, I smile at them. Then they will take an arrow and put arsenic on the tip and strike me, and I smile back?   1995

ON THE MEDIA

There are many ways of putting over one's political points of view. We depend upon the courtesy of the newspapers, and some of them are not very courteous. They go out of their way not to tell the public that you are holding an election meeting because they do not happen to like your political party. They black out one party's meeting, they boost up another's. When one party has a big crowd they say it has a small gathering. If the parties they favour have a small crowd they do not show a picture of the crowd. There are many other ways of manipulating propaganda.   1957

—◦◦◦—

The photographer with his camera is a much more valuable defender of democracy than the soldier or the policeman with a gun.   1962

—◦◦◦—

At the end of the day, it's what we do for our people that counts. And the more they [the Western press] exaggerate our warts and moles and other deficiencies, of which I admit I have many, and I don't try cosmetic techniques to make myself look more presentable than I am, I think the less credible will they become. This is because in a world of very rapid mass communications and mass travel, people are beginning to rely not just on what they read in the newspapers and on what they see on the television screen, but what they actually see for themselves; what their friends whom they trust tell them. As far as investors are concerned – they are more important to me than the Western press and pressmen – it is what the banker and the Ambassador who lives in the country say that makes him decide whether he is going to screw down machinery worth hundreds of millions, sometimes a few billion dollars, to the ground.   1977

One value which does not fit Singapore is the theory of the press as the fourth estate. From British times, the Singapore press was never the fourth estate. And in Singapore's experience, because of our volatile racial and religious mix, the American concept of the 'marketplace of ideas', instead of producing harmonious enlightenment, has time and again led to riots and bloodshed.

1988

—◦—

Singapore's domestic debate is a matter for Singaporeans. We allow American journalists in Singapore in order to report Singapore to their fellow countrymen. We allow their papers to sell in Singapore so that we can know what foreigners are reading about us. But we cannot allow them to assume a role in Singapore that the American media play in America, that of invigilator, adversary and inquisitor of the administration. If allowed to do so, they will radically change the nature of Singapore society, and I doubt if our social glue is strong enough to withstand such treatment. 1988

—◦—

This cultural supremacy is again evident when the American media praises Taiwan, Korea, the Philippines or Thailand for becoming democratic and having a free press. It is praise with condescension, compliments from a superior culture patting an inferior one on the head. And it is this same sense of cultural supremacy which leads the American media to pick on Singapore and beat us up as authoritarian, dictatorial; an over-ruled, over-restricted, stifling, sterile society. Why? Because we have not complied with their ideas of how we should govern ourselves. But we can ill afford to let others experiment with our lives. Their ideas are theories, theories not proven in East Asia, not even in the Philippines after they had governed the Philippines for 50 years. Nor is it proven as yet in Taiwan, or Thailand, or Korea. When it is proven that these countries have become better societies than Singapore, in 5 or 10 years, we will run after them to adopt their practices and try to catch up. 1995

The American press are appalled that I am suing them. But if I didn't sue them I change my relationship with my own people. They sell their newspapers in Singapore, commenting on Singapore, influencing my voters. And if I do not challenge them when they libel me, there will be no end to it. Singapore's newspapers will do likewise. I say if you sell here, you abide by our laws. 1996

—◦—

As East Asia develops, its people will master the media and Asian documentaries and commentators will interpret world events to us from an Asian perspective. There will be a re-affirmation of Asian culture, its traditions and values. 2000

—◦—

Freedom of the press, freedom of the news media, must be subordinated to the overriding needs of Singapore, and to the primacy of purpose of an elected government. 2000

—◦—

In 1977, we passed laws to prohibit any person or his nominee from holding more that 3 per cent of the ordinary shares of a newspaper [...] I do not subscribe to the Western practice that allows a wealthy press baron to decide what voters should read day after day. 2000

—◦—

Why am I so strong against the media? Because they tried to put us down, they twisted everything I said, [they said] that I was a communist. And they knew I wasn't. So I told them, in 1959 during the election campaign as they were gunning for me, I said when I win, I will show you how you have to behave yourself. 2006

ON EQUALITY

We shall strive to establish, by peaceful and constitutional methods, a socialist Malaysia where no man shall be allowed to exploit his fellow man and where all, regardless of race, sex or religion, will be given equal opportunities to contribute their best to society.   1955

⸺⬦⬦⬦⸺

This year will bring Merdeka[1] to Malaya. Let us redouble our efforts to unite all women of all races and all classes in their common fight for a society where women are equal members of the community.   1957

⸺⬦⬦⬦⸺

They [the civil service] must be prepared to compete on equal terms. A system in which because the white man spoke English and therefore he liked best the near-white man who spoke English, and after that the local man who spoke English, cannot be sustained in a situation where the boss has changed. The boss is no longer the Secretary of State for the Colonies. The bosses collectively are the miserable hawkers and labourers, teachers, clerks – the people of Singapore.   1957

⸺⬦⬦⬦⸺

I believe in socialism because I believe it is one of the most effective ways of mobilising human resources. Give equal opportunities to all regardless of rank, race, religion, sex in a given nation and you are likely to draw from each of your nationals, the best in him. Give him the best opportunity to educate himself in order to use his talents, and if you throw your net wide enough to cover your whole population, the chances are you will have ever so much more talent that will emerge to the top.   1966

If we believe in the dignity of man, in his right to live in freedom, if we respect human life, regardless of colour and creed, then we must resist the fatalistic apathy that in the end men, whether in ancient tribes or modern nations, are beasts who seek their own selfish interests to the exclusion, or worse, at the expense of others of the human race. As democratic socialists, within our own countries we reject the proposition that the rich should get richer and the poor should get poorer. We fight economic and social injustice, eradicate unfair practices and create more equal opportunities for all.   1966

We must have tolerance, be forbearing and have respect for one another. But most important, make sure that you have the wherewithal so that the other person will respect you. It is when you have not the wherewithal that you have to plead for equality and respect. The day you have the sinews, the economic foundation, the closely knit social organisation plus the vitality and vigour and the strength of a modern equipped society, that day is the day we can be friendly and we can be equal, and respect will be mutual.   1966

In any given society, of the one thousand babies born, there are so many per cent near-geniuses, so many per cent average, so many per cent morons. I am sorry if I am constantly preoccupied with what the near-geniuses and the above-average are going to do. But I am convinced that it is they who ultimately decide the shape of things to come. It is the above-average in any society who sets the pace. We want an equal society. We want to give everybody equal opportunities. But, at the back of our minds, never deceive ourselves that two human beings are ever equal in their stamina, in their drive, in their dedication, in their innate ability. And my preoccupation is with those who can really make a contribution, who can matter, given the training and the discipline.   1966

It has been government policy to employ girls for all jobs which are physically less demanding, and which girls can do as well as boys. We would ask private firms, wherever possible and practical, to do likewise. Most clerical jobs, service in shops, restaurants and hotels, and light manual work, should be done by girls.

1975

—oo—

Too much 'yin' or equality leads to poor all-round effort and performance. Deng Xiaoping[7] called this the iron-rice-bowl syndrome, which means every worker's rice bowl cannot be broken. In other words, nobody can be sacked, indeed everybody is entitled to equal pay. So there is less and less rice to go into the bowl because no one exerts himself [...] Too much 'yang' or male competitiveness makes each man go for himself alone and risks undermining national solidarity.

1991

—oo—

Singapore's experience has been that once women are educated equally with men and given the same job opportunities, they do not see any point in having large families which drag down the standards of living of the family and of society and make their lives a drudgery.

1993

—oo—

From our earliest days we set out to create a more fair and equal society. We knew we could never achieve complete equality. Human beings are not born equal. They are highly competitive. Systems like Soviet and Chinese communism have failed, because they try to equalise benefits. Then nobody works hard enough, but everyone wants to get as much as, if not more than, the other person. Even welfare socialism has had negative effects on the economy of the UK and EU as the workforce loses the incentives to excel and be better rewarded.

2006

ON IMMIGRATION
AND EMIGRATION

For cheap labour, they [the British] allowed unrestricted immigration without any plan, without any policy and without any intention of creating or preserving the self. I do not condemn the immigration as such, but I condemn the government which has no regard for the people of the country who have been assimilated and did not bother to educate or to provide education for those coming in. Today, with the renaissance of the motherland of each of the immigrant groups, chauvinist tendencies are incited. Yet at this critical juncture we have to call upon these immigrants to give this country their undivided loyalty.

1957

Our progress must not falter through a shortage of skilled workers. We are bringing up to date our educational system and preparing our students with the skills required. Meanwhile, we must allow skilled workers to come in and help us take advantage of this spurt in industrial growth. Hong Kong workers, we have found, will not come, if at the end of five years, after the factory has been established and our own skilled men have been trained, we want them to leave. So whether from Hong Kong or elsewhere, we now offer these skilled artisans permanent residence and, on completion of five years of good work, the opportunity to obtain citizenship.

1970

It is time to bring in work permit holders in the middle ranges of skill and salary scales. Better quality foreign wokers can put the spurs in the hinds of Singaporeans. Liberal immigration policies of skilled and disciplined workers for permanent residence with the view to later citizenship, will make Singaporeans sit up and try harder.

1980

Singaporean teachers feel unhappy at the higher salaries paid to native English teachers. Well, this cannot be avoided. We have to pay them what will bring them to Singapore – the market rate in the UK plus an extra to attract them to Singapore. I frequently meet expat bankers, executives of multinationals, indeed occasionally expat officers working for the Singapore government on contract, who are paid more than I am. I have learned not to let it disturb me.

1980

———✧———

If a brain drain ever happens in Singapore, if our brightest and our best scatter abroad, because of populist appeals to soak or squeeze our able and successful professionals to subsidize those who are less able, less educated, and less well-paid, Singapore will be ruined. The sufferers will be the mass of the workers and their families who cannot emigrate because they are not wanted by the wealthy and developed English-speaking countries. The Singapore-born must be the pillars on which we can place the cross beams and struts of foreign-born talent to raise us up to higher standards of achievement.   1982

———✧———

Unless we are able to instil patriotism and self-respect, unless we succeed in inculcating a sense of commitment to fellow Singaporeans in our talented youths, we can be creamed off. We shall become diluted like skimmed milk. We must ensure that because Singaporeans value their Asianness, they will not want to be tolerated and patronized as minorities in predominantly Caucasian societies. Therefore, any policy which denies trained talent its free-market rewards by punitive taxes, as in Britain, must lead to a brain drain and to our inevitable decline.   1982

It is unrealistic not to recognise that the quality of Ministers, of permanent secretaries, and chairmen and chief executive officers of the statutory boards will be of lower capacity unless we are able to increase the inflow of talent from outside Singapore. The Singapore pool of talent is finite and limited. Singapore has been like the American space shuttle. It has two rockets to boost it into space. We have a powerful Singapore-made rocket. For that extra zip, we had a second rocket, assembled in Singapore, but with imported components. We must try hard to continue to have that second rocket.   1982

———

Singaporeans must realise and accept as desirable the need for more of the able and the talented to come to work in Singapore. We have to compete against the wealthy developed countries who now also recruit such talent. We have to make these people feel welcome and wanted, so that they will make Singapore their permanent home and contribute to the overall progress of all our people [...] They can give that extra boost which has lifted our economy and our society to heights we could not have achieved if we had depended only on Singapore-born talent.   1982

———

We must try to be a bigger business centre for ASEAN businessmen, for the top ASEAN companies, just like Hong Kong. We must make them feel at home. Those of you who have gone to Hong Kong will have seen big commercial buildings with the names of well-known companies from Thailand, Indonesia, the Philippines, Malaysia and Singapore, and not just their airlines. We have to be a cosmopolitan Asian city for all peoples from the world over, Americans, Europeans, Arabs and Asians. We must make these Taiwanese, Chinese, Korean and Japanese businessmen feel welcome in Singapore and encourage them to site their regional HQs here. Then when there is any unusual movement in their capitals, we will have that 'buzz' and that 'electric' in the air.   1997

The more talent we draw into Singapore at all levels, to make up for what we haven't got, the more we will thrive. 2003

———◦◦———

The issue of new citizens and PRs: we have to welcome them. How fast can we integrate them and make them more like us? That depends on us, the citizens born and bred here, and also on their willingness to adapt and be part of our society. 2009

———◦◦———

If we do not have educated Malaysians, China Chinese and India Indians and others from the region, our economy will decline. Our labour force will shrink. In Asia, Japan's fertility rate is 1.37. Their population is ageing and declining, from 120 million to 90 million in 2055. They refuse to accept immigrants, so their economy is feeble and lacks vitality. Without immigration, the ageing problem will be too heavy a burden for our young. Immigrants who can be integrated without upsetting the racial balance are in our interest. 2009

———◦◦———

The economy needs foreign workers, so that we can grow faster when conditions are favourable, and to buffer the shock when conditions turn. This year, many of the job losses have been foreign workers rather than citizens. In fact, among residents (citizens and PRs) there are net job gains in the first half, despite the -6.5% growth! Had we not had the foreign workers, more Singaporeans would have lost their jobs. 2009

The government understands the concerns of Singaporeans over new immigrants and foreign workers. We have taken steps to moderate the inflow and to widen the differentiation between citizens and non-citizens. However, people must recognise that with Singapore's declining population, we need more educated immigrants, including those who have studied or worked in the US and Europe. The majority of the new PRs and citizens are skilled workers and professionals in finance, IT and R&D. They bring new skills, global connections and a strong drive to create better lives for their families. They make us more competitive and dynamic.　　　　2010

⸺∘∘⸺

Some Singaporeans are discomforted by seeing so many strangers around them in the MRT and buses. Please remember, we need the 900,000 foreign workers on two-year work permits. They do the construction and other heavy work, jobs Singaporeans are not willing to do. Their two-year work permits can be extended several times. But they will not stay here permanently.　　2011

ON LANGUAGE

Wise parents will never let their children speak dialect at all. No child, however intelligent, has unlimited data storage capacity. The memory space is finite, be it for words, for facts, or for figures.   1955

———◦◦◦———

Whither are we going? Is it going to be a Malaya with a single language imposed on all its subjects? Or is it going to be a Malaya where various languages are allowed to foster and to flourish, but with a common thread running through them, with one lingua franca, or as the Minister for Housing would have it, one national language? What is to be that lingua franca? These are problems which I think we should seriously start to consider.   1955

———◦◦◦———

It would be stupid for us not to recognise that language and culture is a stronger force that motivates human beings than political or ideological ideals.   1957

———◦◦◦———

It is most important that the problems of language and education be resolved by the free will of the parents, not by the orders of a government. It is our duty to point out the road to national unity by equal opportunities of learning all mother tongues while encouraging the learning and use of the national language [Malay]. Then it is up to the fathers and mothers of our community to decide how their children should be taught and trained.   1961

What I cannot understand, what I don't sympathise with, is the attitude when they say, 'Well, look, if I learn Malay then my son or my daughter will be less Chinese or less Indian.' I say that's nonsense. The Maori speaks English, but he is not less Maori, you know. He is what he is, and he keeps that part of him. So I say, we lose nothing, if we try and seek a common language; and through that common language ultimately we will become a common nation with one cultural milieu to bind its peoples through history and a common experience.

1965

I learnt as a student that a word has three meanings: what the speaker intends it to mean; what the mass of people understand it to mean; what I understand it to mean.

1967

Go to English schools, learn English. But, at the same time, never forget that you are not an Englishman, and I am not an Englishman. English is a language we learn and we use it. But we must keep a part of ourselves – the part that leads us back to our histories, to our cultures, to our civilisations from whence we came and out of that, the past, we will together create a present and a future worthy of a people that have come from very ancient cultures and civilisations.

1967

If you read, and you understand only the English language, then you are at a very grave disadvantage because you really don't know what is going on in a large part of Singapore. If you believe that the *Straits Times* and the *New Nation* is what Singapore is about, then you are living in a dream world.

1976

The difference between my children and me is that when I switch to Mandarin I am like an old valve radio – you know, the old valve radio or TV? The difference between a transistor TV and a valve TV? An old valve TV, once you switch on, takes two to three minutes to warm up. Then you get the sound. Then you get into the mood. Then you switch on to a new circuit, from AC to DC, from 220 volts to 110 volts. But with my children, you switch on, you just press the button, it is on instantly.

1977

—◦◦—

If you lose that Chinese education and you go completely English-educated, you will lose that drive, that self-confidence. That is what is wrong. The danger is, if you are Chinese-educated and only Chinese-educated, you are monolingual, then your source of literature will be communist.

1977

—◦◦—

We will never completely and finally settle the problems of our bilingual and bicultural society. There is always an undercurrent of competition for dominance between languages and cultures. Our special circumstances lead us rationally to accept the fact that English is the working language of our society. However, we all want the culture, values and philosophy of life to remain dominant over that of America, Britain or other parts of the English-speaking world. This requires that we know enough of our own mother tongues to appreciate our own traditions and approach to life.

1978

—◦◦—

From my observation, the monolinguist is more likely to be a language chauvinist and a bigot. He only sees the world through one eye. He does not have binocular vision to see the world in depth, to realise that there are as rich, if not richer, worlds of human experience and knowledge, all expressed in beautiful words, elegantly, vividly and fluently in other languages. He does not understand other great civilisations which have expressed themselves in other languages.

1978

The bilinguist sees both sides. A bilingual Chinese Singaporean knows that there was deep wisdom in Chinese culture and philosophy, a result of 4,000 years of periods of great achievements and in between long years of chaos and disaster, through wars and foreign conquests, plagues, floods, drought and famine. At the same time, he is also aware that the ritualised, conformist approach to thinking and learning, which was designed to secure the stability of successive dynasties, had prevented innovations in human thought and the discovery of further inventions. The result was that a great civilisation had become stagnant. It failed to rejuvenate itself in time to face the strength of an industrialised Europe.   1978

———◦○◦———

It is absurd that so many who have been to Chinese school give up using Mandarin and are more fluent in Hokkien. To watch RTS[8] features showing our workers, who obviously have gone to Chinese schools, speaking halting Mandarin is painful. It is a grave loss to themselves and our society. If in the factories and workshops the usage had been Mandarin between the workers, we would be a better, more united, a more cultivated and educated people.

1978

———◦○◦———

With a 75 per cent Chinese majority in Singapore, it is easy to work up Chinese sentiments and to get power on the strength of the Chinese vote. We eschewed the tactic. And we stopped others from doing so. Instead, we persuaded the Chinese to accept bilingualism with English as the first language.   1987

We need a common language. We solved this by making everybody learn not one but two languages, English and the mother tongue. English is not any group's mother tongue, so no advantage is gained or lost by any one group. We have neither forced nor pressure-cooked a national identity. We have refrained from suppressing ethnic culture, languages, religions or sense of identity.

1993

<hr>

I expected that the Chinese press would decline over the years because our education policy emphasised English, but it hasn't. The emotional attachment is very deep, especially of the working classes to the language of their homes.

1995

<hr>

Because my children did not speak it [Mandarin] at home, I sent them to Chinese schools where the language environment was Chinese and the discipline was more rigorous with the emphasis on courtesy, humility and character-building. They have benefited from their Chinese school education.

1997

<hr>

Let me state clearly the disadvantages of Singlish. There are as many varieties of English as there are communities that speak English. In spite of differences in accent and pronunciation, people in Britain, America, Canada, Australia and New Zealand understand each other easily because they are speaking the same language, using the same words with the same grammar and sentence structures. Singaporeans add Chinese and Malay words into Singlish, and give different meanings to English words like 'blur' to mean 'blank'. Worse, Singlish uses Chinese sentence structure. In fact we are creating a different, new language. Each family can create its own coded language; nothing wrong with that except that no one outside the family can understand you. We are learning English so that we can understand the world and the world can understand us.

1999

What is the responsibility of the government? It is, first and foremost, to give everyone enough English language skills to make a living. Because if he cannot make a living, nothing else is important. However, we also need to teach him his mother tongue, because that is what gives him his identity and makes our society vigorous and distinctive.   2004

———◦○◦———

I paid a heavy price for not having learned Mandarin when young. To this day I meet my teacher/friend once a week to keep my Mandarin alive. Every day I spend 20 minutes listening to Mandarin lessons on tape and 15 minutes reading *ZaoBao*, or Chinese newspapers online. These keep up my passive vocabulary.   2004

———◦○◦———

To keep a language alive, you have to speak and read it frequently. The more you use one language, the less you use other languages. So the more languages you learn, the greater the difficulties of retaining them at a high level of fluency. I have learned and used six languages – English, Malay, Latin, Japanese, Mandarin and Hokkien. English is my master language. My Hokkien has gone rusty, my Mandarin has improved. I have lost my Japanese and Latin, and can no longer make fluent speeches in Malay without preparation. This is called 'language loss'.   2009

ON RACE

We, I think, unlike the colonial government, cannot afford to ignore basic likes and dislikes – basic facts. One of these basic facts is that no racial or linguistic group in this country will give up its own language, its own culture, its own traditions, completely for either English or any other Anglicized form of Malayan language, culture or tradition.   1955

In multiracial Malaya with three major races – Malays, Chinese and Indians – all with differing cultural and linguistic backgrounds, and even more important, with different political traditions and concepts, the dictatorship of any one party may lead to racial conflict and disaster.   1957

Malaya's most acute problem at present is communalism. The easiest emotions to arouse in any group of people are their oneness in race, culture, language and religion. And it is a temptation too strong to resist for political adventurers to make an appeal to these emotions to win support. So we must hail the defeat of Dato Onn in the Batu Pahat by-elections, in a predominantly Malay area where he made the greatest call to communalism ever to the Malays. And we must cheer the victory of the PAP Malay candidate, Inche Baharuddin bin Mohamed Ariff in the Crawford division of the Singapore City Council elections, where in a predominantly Chinese division in a predominantly Chinese city, he got the biggest majority of any candidate in the Singapore elections, in spite of the Chinese communal line taken by his opponents.   1958

I think we can safely predict that in two decades, either there [will be] a tolerant multiracial society comprising us in this region, or this will be an area of constant strife, very much like what the Balkan States were before and after the First World War.   1965

—⦾—

The problem is how to create a situation where the minority, either in ethnic, linguistic or religious terms, is not conscious that it is a minority; where the exercise of its rights as an equal citizen is so natural and so accepted a part of our society that it is not conscious of the fact that it is sharing, within this wider whole, equal rights with the dominant ethnic groups who accept its equality as a matter of fact.   1966

—⦾—

Every time I think of people whom I have met and known as friends in school or in college, I think of those who became too de-culturalised too quickly. I had a friend who was a Sikh. He threw his past away: he shaved his beard; he threw away his turban; he had a haircut. No harm at all. But something happened to him and in next to no time, he was doing foolish things. He lost his anchorage. You know, it gets very difficult for a ship without an anchor in a harbour when it gets stormy. I want you therefore, to have your anchorage. But slowly, we must begin to learn to have the same basic points of anchorage. It may take a hundred years.   1967

—⦾—

Whatever our race or religion, it is what we produce that entitles us to what we get, not our race or religion. Developing the economy, increasing productivity, increasing returns, these make sense only when fair play and fair shares make it worth everyone's while to put in his share of effort for group survival and group prosperity.   1969

White racist-supremist theories can only be demolished by clearly
demonstrating that the whites are not superior.   1971

———◦———

It is necessary to remind our young that when we started in 1954, and when
we formed the government in 1959, we did not have the basic elements to
be a nation. The attributes of nationhood were missing: a common ethnic
identity – we will never have ethnic homogeneity – but we did not even
have a common ethnic identity; we saw ourselves as disparate Hokkiens,
Cantonese, Hakkas, Teochews, Hainanese. The Chinese Chamber of
Commerce, up till recently, was structured along those lines. And the Malays
were either Malays or Boyanese or Javanese or Minangkabau. They still
have associations to bind people of the same ethnic origins. We did not
have a common language. We couldn't speak to each other. Nor did we have
a common experience, a common sharing of historic events that creates a
common culture.   1980

———◦———

Communalists and religious fanatics can, from time to time, work up racial
and religious passions and ordinary people can be carried along. We cannot
have our minority races worked up and pitted in hatred or fear against the
majority, or have one religion so zealous for converts, or so intolerant, that
they have open friction with other religions. Any communal or religious
collision will be nasty and costly. Our history is besplattered with such
outbursts.   1987

———◦———

We shall need another one to two generations before our national unity is
able to stand severe racial or religious stress. Nationhood cannot be achieved
by pressure-cooking.   1987

Last year, some English-educated intellectuals suggested that we should blur and erase our ethnic, linguistic and cultural differences to speed up nation-building. I believe this is neither realistic nor practical. People will resist such a policy, and by their resistance they will accentuate inter-ethnic differences […] The Chinese must draw on their traditional values in Confucianism, Taoism and Chinese folklore to complement them. The Malays must draw on Malay custom and Islam, the Hindus on their customs and the Hindu religion. If we try to put all these different background cultures into a blenderiser, we will end up with a non-descript melange.   1991

———◦◦———

After two or three generations away from China, we have become rooted in the country of our birth. Our stakes are in our home countries, not China where our ancestors came from. The Chinese Thai is a Thai and in the end he wants Thailand to prosper so that his assets in Thailand can grow and his children's future in Thailand can be secure. So too Chinese Singaporeans, Chinese Indonesians, Chinese Malaysians and Chinese Filipinos. They may invest and visit China frequently, but few want to make China their home.

1993

———◦◦———

Each group that came here carried its own ancestral memories. The Chinese remember the Emperor and the magistrates who represented him. To this day, the majority of Chinese Singaporeans do not want to be actively involved in political parties. It's not in their culture. What they want is to have somebody governing them well and producing things that they want. But if you ask them to stand up and be counted, they'll say, 'I'd rather do that secretly when I vote'. But that doesn't prevent others from coming out. But you will notice the Indians have a different tradition. They love contention, they love argument. So, the majority of our Opposition have always been Indians.   1995

We have made considerable progress in integrating our different races into living in the same housing blocks and going to the same schools and serving in the same SAF units. Now we must aim at more socialising between them, whether in private or community-organised activities. Progress will depend on how comfortable our young feel about each other. The more they socialise, the stronger our mosaic of national cohesion. It is not easy, but it can be done.

1999

———⊸∘⊷———

At present, no MP, Chinese, Malay or Indian, can afford to take a communal line because he has to serve a multiracial constituency. Race-based politics [would] pull apart our society as parties contest to better advance their own community interests.

2001

———⊸∘⊷———

Singapore has a Chinese majority, but whatever your race if you join us as citizens, we accord you equal rights and equal opportunities. This is why we have been able to have considerable inflows of skilled and educated Chinese, Indians, Europeans and others. Because Singapore is an open cosmopolitan society that accepts and welcomes talent, so we have continued to thrive and prosper.

2004

———⊸∘⊷———

Singapore is a multiracial meritocracy. Our neighbours organise their societies on the supremacy of the indigenous peoples, Bumiputras in Malaysia and Pribumis in Indonesia. Though our neighbours have accepted us as a sovereign and independent nation, they have a tendency to externalise towards us their internal anxieties and angst against their own minorities. This is unlikely to go away.

2009

ON RELIGION

All great religions of the world preach universal brotherhood regardless of race, language and culture. In a world growing ever smaller by man's conquest of air and space, in travel and communications, no religion or ideology can ignore the diversity in the social mores, the habits and customs, the different histories of the many peoples of this world.   1968

❧

However different the various religions, this government is in favour of a man believing in something [rather] than believing in nothing. I would rather have a Muslim, a devout Hindu, than a permissive atheist. And it is because of the problem of atheism in the West that they are in trouble.   1977

❧

A distinctive feature of the Hindu religion and culture is its tolerance for other religions and cultures. All major world religions and cultures meet in Singapore. The values and traditions of Christian charity, Islamic brotherhood, Confucian ethics, and the Buddhist's search for enlightenment, are all part of Singapore's spiritual milieu. Everyone knows that virtue is not exclusive to any religion. As long as we preach and practise tolerance and harmony and freedom of religion, we shall continue to be at peace with ourselves and to make progress.   1978

❧

The observance of the fast during Ramadan requires discipline and fortitude of Muslims. In a multi-religious society it is an example of how we can accommodate each other in the different religious practices. We can accord dignity to each other's spiritual lives.   1980

We must match our economic progress with advances in the moral, ethical and aesthetic dimensions of our life. The established religions have an important role to play in our moral and spiritual development. We expanded the teaching of religious knowledge subjects to all our schools from 1984. And the government is completely neutral between the different religions. Singaporeans can decide for themselves.   1987

—◦—

Religion must not get mixed up in politics, otherwise a clash of political views can easily turn into a clash of religious beliefs. Then there will be deep enmity between our different religious communities and our society will come to grief.   1987

—◦—

Religion cannot be a force for national unity. Indeed, secularism is essential for inter-religious harmony for our multi-religious community.   1990

—◦—

It is necessary to emphasise that the war against terrorism is not a war against Islam. The majority of Muslims have nothing to do with terrorism or extremism. However, militant terrorists groups have hijacked Islam as their driving force and have given it a virulent twist. Throughout the Muslim world, the militants are out to impose their version of Islam.   2002

ON INTERNATIONAL
RELATIONS

When the first Russian Sputnik spun in the sky in September last year, it symbolised a new scientific and technological era, man's conquest of nature [...] But instead of bringing joy and jubilation to the whole world, this achievement brought fear and gloom to one half of the world. The Americans have made frantic efforts to launch their own satellite, spurned on by fear of being conquered or destroyed by Russian-manned satellites. Man may have conquered space, but he has not learned to conquer his own primeval instincts and emotions which were necessary for his survival in the Stone Age, not in the Space Age.   1958

No people like to be told by their neighbours, particularly a smaller one, what they should do about their leaders.   1963

If it is wrong that a man should exploit his fellow men, so it is wrong that a rich nation or a group of rich nations should exploit the poorer group of nations. If it is unjust and economically backward and old-fashioned to allow a man through his possession of property or status to exploit his less fortunate fellow men, then by the same token no nation or group of nations should be allowed through their possession of industrial capital and technological skills and scientific knowledge to exploit other groups of nations, who, through the accidents of history, have not got these essentials for development.   1966

Why should developed nations give two per cent or even one per cent of their Gross National Product to aid the development of underdeveloped countries, many of whom are politically awkward to the West, some of whom have corrupt regimes, and nearly all of whom are not publicly grateful for assistance which they have come to expect as of right?   1966

———◦◦———

We want the maximum number of friends and the minimum number of enemies, and naming anybody as an enemy is the surest way of making him your enemy.   1968

———◦◦———

What has happened in Vietnam is a precursor of what will happen in other parts of the world unless countries within themselves can eradicate or lessen the tensions which internal inequalities, gross odious inequalities of wealth and opportunity, generate into hatred and bitterness and finally insurgency and revolution.   1975

———◦◦———

We have had to live with not-so-rational leaders in the past. When Sukarno mounted 'Confrontation' against Malaysia (including Singapore) from 1963, we depended on the British to defend us. 'Confrontation' ended in 1966 only because a rational leader in President Suharto took over.   1987

———◦◦———

Satellite pictures transmitted into our living rooms vividly and nightly remind us of the troubled world we live in. The gap between the rich and the poor remains vast. The Commonwealth is probably one of the few settings in which rich and poor countries can meet and talk to each other candidly.   1989

To have influence, Japan has to become more international-minded, more outward going in her outlook and less self-centred, more open and hospitable to foreigners, especially to fellow Asians, who rank low in Japanese esteem. A society which is courteous but not warm and friendly is not so readily accepted, admired and emulated.

1991

⸺◦⸺

Fear of Japan's re-militarisation is more emotional than rational. But it is a reality that influences attitudes in many East Asian countries, not only towards the remote eventuality of a Japanese invasion, but also towards the more likely possibility of Japan assuming a wider security role in the region.

1992

⸺◦⸺

Unfortunately, unlike the Germans, Japan has not been open and frank about the atrocities and horrors committed in World War II. By avoiding to talk about it, the victims suspect and fear that Japan does not think these acts were wrong, and that there is no genuine Japanese change of heart.

1992

⸺◦⸺

The Americans are great missionaries. They have an irrepressible urge to convert others.

1992

⸺◦⸺

The world may be divided into nations, but no longer is any nation impervious to contact, infiltration and influence by others. We have become one interacting, interdependent world. Whether it is global warming, the ozone layer over the Arctic, or nuclear fallout, or the population bomb, the problems besetting the world are transnational and the solutions must be transnational.

1992

If the Ramos Administration can make ordinary Filipinos understand that politics is not simply elections with singing, fiestas and giveaways, but that it is about their lives, jobs and wages, homes, schools and hospitals, the situation can change dramatically. When ordinary Filipinos know that the country's stagnation and their joblessness is because of vested interests, corrupt politics and general disorder and lack of confidence, they will agitate in support of those who want to establish law and order and discipline, cut high tariffs, quotas to licensing and other restrictive monopolistic practices, in order to get investments to give them jobs.

1992

—◦◦—

Attitudes are changing. Worldwide satellite television makes it increasingly difficult for any government to hide its cruelties to its own people. By international convention what a government does with its own people is an internal matter and does not concern foreign governments. This convention is difficult to uphold when people worldwide see and condemn the cruelties and want something done to stop them. On the other hand, Western governments often use public opinion as an excuse to interfere with another government's actions. But are Western governments prepared to help financially to ease the severe economic difficulties which are often the cause of upheavals and their suppression by force? Only if they are, do they have a moral right to interfere and to be listened to.

1992

—◦◦—

Americans are in a political malaise. Their academics and commentators know and publicly discuss their problems. But there is no political will in either the Republican or Democratic party to get American voters to face the facts of life, namely that they are living beyond their means and that to regain competitiveness, they must cut spending, especially on welfare, increase savings and investments, improve education, and improve work attitudes, before consumption can be allowed to go up again.

1992

A US-style constitution failed [in the Philippines] long before Marcos declared martial law. It was re-adopted in 1987 by President Aquino. The system worked in America because of a super-abundance of resources and riches in a vast underpopulated continent. I do not believe that Korea, Taiwan, Hong Kong or Singapore could have succeeded as they have done if they had to work under such a constitution, where gridlock on every major issue is a way of life. And you will notice that since the Vietnam War and the Great Society some 28 years ago, the US system has not functioned even for the United States.   1992

East Asia should get together, not to build another regional bloc, but to work for closer economic ties between themselves and the US and Canada, and when the North American Free Trade Agreement (NAFTA) is ratified, with NAFTA. Closer association between East Asian countries and NAFTA will check tendencies towards an inward-looking NAFTA. The long-term aim should be a free trade agreement amongst APEC members. In other words, convert NAFTA in stages into PAFTA, the Pacific Asia Free Trade Area. 1993

The dynamic but still poor countries in East Asia presently seek peaceful outlets for their energies. If they are denied outlets through trade and investments, their energies will eventually lead to conflicts and war. For example, every Chinese knows from the *Romance of the Three Kingdoms* that in ancient China, the time-honoured method for a more dynamic and vigorous people to achieve greater wealth and prosperity was to incorporate chunks of neighbouring territories and peoples into their kingdom. Then the victor has a wider range of soils, climates and peoples, a wider base for wealth through exchanges of a greater diversity of goods and services.   1993

To be part of the Asian dynamic, Australians do not need to become Asians, in culture, in values or in habits. But it is necessary for Australians to understand Asians, to feel at ease with Asians, and to make Asians feel at ease with them so that they can all work together comfortably and on equal terms. This is not possible if Australians do not quite accept Asians, or are disdainful of those with different values or habits.   1994

—◦◦—

If Japan is to be a world player in the field of economic and politics, it has to become an open society like the US, easy to read and understand. It must win the respect and admiration of other countries. Japan cannot hold itself out as a unique civilisation. Instead, Japan has to become a model from which others can borrow parts of Japanese civilisation to improve their own system and so be more successful. This needs a profound change in the mindset of Japanese leaders and especially those in politics, the media and academia.   1994

—◦◦—

If the US tries to thwart China's growth, China will surely want to return the compliment when it can do so.   1994

—◦◦—

What happens in China, Japan and the rest of East Asia will decide the kind of world we live in. It's best for the world not to repeat the errors of imperial preferences and beggar-thy-neighbour policies of currency devaluations that led to World War II. The world has become too integrated by science and technology to be kept divided by ideology, religion, culture or race. We have become one interdependent and mutually destructible world.   1994

There is no way for Asia by itself, without America, to find a balance. If you remove the Americans from the equation, even if you combine Japan and Korea, the other countries in Southeast Asia, Vietnam, ASEAN, Australia, New Zealand, they still can't balance China. The difference in weight is disproportionate, unless the Japanese decide to become nuclear and rearm in a big way. That would be a very dangerous world. So, the future depends very much on maintaining an American presence in the region, which I believe is likely to continue for some while because they're joining in the growth.   1995

———⟨∘⟩———

This generation of Asians, especially the leaders, have learned their lesson: whatever your quarrels, if you go to war, you will be pauperized. By all means, let's argue, but at the end of the day let's work together. Let's trade. Let's get on with it. You grow, I grow. That's the best.   1996

———⟨∘⟩———

The China-Japan relationship is the most difficult to manage. It is not easy for Japan and China to have a 'normal' relationship. Proximity and history complicate their relationship. Nevertheless, Japan and China are complementary with each other. Japan has the technology and capital that China needs for its development. China offers Japan the markets. The obstacle is history, whose legacy of suspicions can stunt the growth of a relationship that could benefit both.   1996

———⟨∘⟩———

Japan's best investment is in the younger generation of potential leaders of China. The more Chinese students there are in Japan, especially the children of central and provincial leaders, the better the prospects for long-term understanding and cooperation between the two countries.   1996

Americans are not criticising Singapore because they are concerned about democracy and human rights enjoyed by three million Singaporeans. Whether Singapore succeeds as a multiracial community in Southeast Asia or fails makes little difference to the future of America. Their real interest is what Freedom House has stated, that Singapore sets the wrong example for China, showing China that it can maintain social discipline and order with high economic growth but without becoming a full-fledged American-style democracy. This is the reason why the American media always attacks Singapore.   1997

—∘—

The Western gloss that gives that cosmopolitan air to Hong Kong will gradually be worn away by constant exchanges with China. Hong Kong's leaders will subconsciously revert to their Chinese cultural reflexes. There will be a blending of their present different social mores. This underlines the need for Hong Kong to have a strong-minded and firm chief executive, supported by a non-corrupt and efficient civil service, to preserve the virtues of the British system: the rule of law and the sanctity of contracts, fair commercial practices, a level playing field between all players whether they be well-connected insiders or unconnected outsiders, and transparency and accountability in all decision-making.   1997

I have taken a deep interest in both China and India ever since I started my political life in 1950. Like all democratic socialists of the 1950s, I have tried to analyse and forecast which giant would make the grade. I had hoped it would be democratic India, not communist China. By the 1980s I had become more realistic and accepted the differences between the two. It is simplistic to believe that democracy and free markets are the formula that must lead to progress and wealth. However, I am convinced the contrary axiom is true: that central planning and state-owned or nationalised enterprises lead to inefficiency and poor returns, whether the government is authoritarian or democratic. Moreover, even if China and India were both democratic, or authoritarian or communist, their performance would be different. I now believe that, besides the standard economic yardsticks for productivity and competitiveness, there are intangible factors like culture, religion and other ethnic characteristics and national ethos that affect the outcome. 2005

A small country must seek a maximum number of friends, while maintaining the freedom to be itself as a sovereign and independent nation. Both parts of the equation – a maximum number of friends and freedom to be ourselves – are equally important and interrelated. Friendship, in international relations, is not a function of goodwill or personal affection. We must make ourselves relevant so that other countries have an interest in our continued survival and prosperity as a sovereign and independent nation. 2009

ON SECURITY

It is difficult to rob a weaker man if he has strong friends prepared and able to give the robber a hiding.   1956

—◇—

Awards [scholarships] are given to persons on the basis of merit, not whether they are pro or against any political party. But where a person is deemed a security risk to the State, where his political beliefs are of such a nature as to constitute a risk, then it is not the business of the state to give money to such people in order to help them undermine the State. But these policies are interpreted very liberally. [...] We do not want to make a man more embittered and more frustrated with society than he need be. If he has youthful inclinations towards extreme political views, well, by all means, let him go through that phase; let him mature. But when we know a man is already committed to the destruction of the democratic State, it is not our business to spend money on him to equip him to carry out his purposes better.   1964

—◇—

We are not naive enough to believe that the British, the Australians and the New Zealanders come to our aid purely for reasons of charity, humanity, and love of democracy. Of course, the British would like to keep their economic interests in this region. Of course, they want to keep a foothold – if not a foothold at least a toehold – for their military interests and military influence to extend over this area. And, of course, they want to keep their lines open with New Zealand and Australia. But the acid question is: is it in our interest and the collective interest of nearly 11 million Malaysians to have them fighting on our behalf, or out of this country with us fighting on our own?   1964

I have got a little island with the highest standard of living in the whole of Asia outside Japan. It is like a suburban villa just placed in a tenement area with a very flimsy fence, and outside are a lot of hungry people and angry people who are being worked up by all kinds of oratory; and they are looking into my orchard, seeing pineapples, bananas, papayas, rambutans you know, our equivalent of pears and peaches they are seeing television sets; nice new two-piece suits, latest styles, the best tailoring out in Southeast Asia; refrigerators filled with milk and honey. And all that I have got is two battalions, and the Indonesians have got 400,000 armed men.   1965

I will tell you why we do not want professional soldiers. This place must learn to live and work for a living. And if you are only a soldier, you do not contribute to the productivity of the place.   1967

We will defend ourselves. Whoever else wants to defend us, I will say to them 'Thank you very much. But please remember I can defend myself and make no mistake about it.'   1968

Unlike many other countries in the area, we form a very compact and neat target, and therefore a sneak aerial attack is a major preoccupation of any Defence Minister of Singapore. It is therefore our intention to ensure that such a sneak attack can never succeed.   1968

If people believe that we will stand up and fight for ourselves, they are more likely to leave us in peace. Hence the phrase 'we fight for peace'. When 'we seek and sue for peace' then we've had it. When we are prepared to fight for it, then we get it.   1968

From time to time in the history of human civilisations, more civilised, more cultivated societies, with higher standards of living, have been overrun and subjugated by barbaric and less advanced groups. So the Roman Empire fell. And so successive Chinese and Indian civilisations were conquered by virile warrior races, who were socially and culturally of a cruder order, and less sophisticated in their social organisations. We must be on our toes all the time. We must never allow this to happen to Singapore through our growing self-indulgent and soft.   1968

—◦—

Whether we are shirkers or quitters, or stayers and fighters, will determine whether we live in peace or not. If people believe that we are stayers and fighters, we are more likely to live peacefully. Next year I hope to see my own son in uniform present on such an occasion. Nobody who is fit and able-bodied can shirk what is a responsibility and an honour, to see that Singapore thrives and prosper, and is left undisturbed and at peace.   1970

—◦—

To survive, we have to be fairly hard-headed people. We cannot afford a large standing army. We cannot afford a large army in a crisis. To have a defence capability, which others will not believe is just for show, we have to develop considerable reserves. At the press of the button, these reserves must form up, with a high degree of combat readiness, practised in the use of all their weapons, from the rifle, to the mortar, to the recoilless guns, and so on. Every passing year sees a new batch, trained and emotionally prepared for this kind of life.   1971

—◦—

We stand for the security of Singapore which unfortunately demands that hard-core detainees who refuse to abjure the use of violence will have to be detained. If they will denounce the use of force to take office, or just to live peacefully – even if they don't support a government – we are happy to save expenses in having to feed them and care for them.   1976

After separation in 1965, we immediately built up our armed forces. Security is crucial to the survival of any people. Without the SAF, all that we have is at risk. Anyone, even random terrorists, can hold us up to ransom. However, opposition parties want to abolish National Service, or reduce it to a community service. Are they out of their minds?

1976

—◦◦◦—

Civilisation is fragile. It is especially so for an island city-state.

1982

—◦◦◦—

New weapons must be bought, younger men must be better educated to handle more advanced weapons. More important, they must have able and resolute leaders. Security is like electricity. It can be stored but not for long.

1982

—◦◦◦—

We do not consider our neighbours in Southeast Asia to be threats to our security. There will always be differences in national interests and perceptions but, so long as the governments and leaders of Southeast Asia are rational, these differences will not lead to armed conflict. The external threats to our security are likely to come from irrational and extremist forces, or from expansionist regimes backed by a big power.

1987

—◦◦◦—

Our basic approach is never to allow fears and tensions to grow and mount in intensity. Early preventive action can forestall an ugly build-up. So whether it is a communist conspiracy to create pressure points for mass action, or growing interracial or inter-religious frictions and tension, they have to be defused early.

1987

The world can become a safer place only when an aggressor who invades another, especially a weaker country, is punished, not rewarded.   1990

—∘—

If I am sure that if I belong to a pack that's got a big dog, I would consider a nip. If we are all small dogs, it may be wiser just to bark.   1995

—∘—

We have to accept the reality that there is no combination of forces in ASEAN that could stand up to a military confrontation with China. Unless there is an outside force, such as America, there can be no balance in the region.   1996

—∘—

These are realities we have to weigh when deploying anyone to a sensitive appointment in the SAF. We must never put the person in a situation where he may face a conflict of loyalties. I said in answer to a question some nearly two years ago that it is a difficult matter to put a Malay Muslim of deeply religious family background in charge of a machine-gun. We should never have to ask this of anyone. Some of you were disturbed by my frankness. But when I faced crises in the 1960s I could not afford to be wrong. Was this discrimination or was it common sense – a policy of prudence?   2001

—∘—

I ask myself, what is the most, the greatest danger to humankind? I think the human being because we have so conquered nature that we are interfering with its capability to sustain itself. Earth warming is a problem, storms in Europe where you never had storms before in northern Europe, droughts in many countries. Whenever there is an El Nino or El Nina, it is the result of indiscriminate growth and use of fossil fuels which is in turn the result of massive increases in population.   2003

ON COMMUNISM

If people are faced with the alternative of a continuation of the colonial system, however streamlined, and a communist Malaya, which is going to be effective and honest even if it is rigid and disciplined and illiberal, I fear that a large mass of the people, who have not the time to bother about liberal concepts of the freedom of the individual – liberty, freedom from arrest without trial, the right of free speech – because they are too preoccupied with making a living, would choose communism.   1955

⎯⎯∞⎯⎯

I cannot in all honesty say that communism is a diabolical evil, because I can imagine certain human societies where it was a great relief to have the communists displace a ruling power. That is another of the very difficult problems we face in this country. To some 600 million Chinese, that philosophy was the answer and is the answer to a decadent, a corrupt and an evil society which has become evil because men have lost their self-respect and lost their values.   1955

⎯⎯∞⎯⎯

I believe that whether we go communist or non-communist in the future depends on whether we can build up a clean, healthy political movement with clean and healthy leaders, men who believe in democracy and social justice and who enter politics because they want to serve and not because they want to loot. If you can find enough such men, honest, able and prepared to work, you can fight the communists without guns. If you cannot, then you resort to SEATO[9], to atom bombs and to hydrogen bombs.   1955

The communists failed because it was a propaganda based on the barricade, and you get men running to the barricades only if they are really hungry, really desperate. Then, they are prepared to take up the stone, throw it into the glass window, turn the car over and burn it. When they are not desperate, when they are reasonably fed, reasonably clothed, I won't say contented, but not altogether frustrated and dissatisfied, then argument and reason become operative factors. 1962

I would put the problem of visiting communist countries simply in this way. It is utter stupidity to allow communists, local communists, to go abroad to seek instruction on methods of subversion and intrigue and to receive inspiration for their flagging morale. I think it is not part of my job to go and help them to carry out the communist revolution successfully. In fact, it's my job to see that the stupidities and the blunders that they have committed fall heavily upon their heads. 1962

If a man has something to live for – if today he has a bicycle and is earning enough, feeding his family in nice and decent surroundings, and with enough to buy a scooter on the hire purchase – from the bicycle he goes to the scooter – that is tangible progress. And he would not listen to all this wild and silly talk of revolution and violence. And if from the scooter he is doing well enough to go to one of the Mini-Minor cars – there is the 500, the 600, the Mini Cooper which is revved up and can do 100 mph – he can take a girlfriend out for a spin, that is reasonable and tolerable. After all, that is what they are fighting for even in a communist society and even in Moscow. 1962

Communism, like so many other things, is best met when one knows it and gets immune to it. I believe the policy of complete isolation from communist thought, tactics, thinking, policy, is a dangerous thing. One day the windows will come open and like the South Sea islanders, when they first meet the tuberculosis bacilli, we will all perish. It is better to let these things come in gradual doses, containable, enough to generate a counter toxin in our wholesome society.   1964

We in Singapore were startled by the sharp clash between two communist states to our north, for the time being confined to the Indo-Chinese Peninsula. We were startled because we could not believe one communist government had set out deliberately to subvert and overthrow another communist government. When a communist does this to a non-communist government, he calls it 'liberation'. When he does it to another communist government, he calls it 'salvation'.   1978

I always take a communist leader at face value. If he tells his people, in his official organs, his press, his radio, his books and his publications, that the world will become communist because it is the inevitable march of history, then I must take that seriously at face value. It is his intention to help history. I have never allowed myself to be bemused to the contrary.   1978

Seventy years in the Soviet Union of the egalitarian society, have they banished beggary, prostitution, misery, hunger? Is that the way, to suppress the individual instinct to perform, to excel, to be better than the other, to get better rewards, bigger prizes, to increase his family's chances in life, so that they can have a better kick-off? All that was stifled with the objective of an equal egalitarian society.   1989

Once upon a time, in the 1950s, many Singaporeans, especially the Chinese-educated, believed that China was a stupendous success in instant revolution and industrialisation, arising from glossy magazines and brilliant broadcasts of production figures and spick-and-span showpieces for distinguished visitors to be taken to, children's palaces, model factories, model villages. I believe the majority of young Singaporeans or young Chinese in Singapore in the 1950s would have voted for that system. That is the danger of one man, one vote. It was a mirage. It was a con job. We knew it only in the 1970s and it became obvious to everyone in the 1980s.   1989

—◦◦—

Forty-five years of competition against the West has broken the Soviet Union and her cluster of Marxist states. They cannot match the productive abundance, the comforts and technological excellence of the capitalist economies of the West. Suddenly they have decided to disclose their industrial backwardness. Never has there been so propitious a moment in history. A new dispensation offering rich prizes to countries is now within grasp. The East Europeans have abandoned their failed system and want to take the path that led Western Europe to prosperity and freedom.   1990

—◦◦—

The communist ideology no longer holds the Chinese people in thrall. No Chinese in China any longer believes that communism is the wave of the future. They know of the Chinese in Taiwan and Hong Kong and want to be as prosperous as them.   1992

ON CHINA

China cannot revert to closed-door policies. When the veterans of the Long March leave the scene, their successors will have to prove their legitimacy, and their right to govern will depend on their ability to rapidly improve the lives of the Chinese people.

1990

The problem for China is how to accommodate the desire of their educated and knowledgeable people in the cities to decide how they should be governed. These are people who are well informed about other societies, including Taiwan and Hong Kong. But the 900 million peasants have different priorities and concerns. One man, one vote for 1,100 million Chinese to choose a President, a Congress or a Senate, will lead to chaotic results. But then neither can a self-perpetuating Communist Party claim to represent the people.

1991

Can the habits and values of Chinese governance of over 4,000 years be changed overnight by resolutions of the US Congress? I believe change will come to China. But it will be an internally generated process of evolution.

1992

In China the laws are incomplete and rules and procedures not transparent. A 'level playing field' is not part of Chinese culture; *guanxi* or personal links is.

1992

If China's brightest and best are exposed to other cultures through studying in the US, Japan and Europe, they must become less ethnocentric. They will realise that the planet Earth is very small, very interdependent and very vulnerable; that a stable world needs a strong set of rules to govern the behaviour of big and small countries and that military force is too destructive when others are nearly as powerful. 1994

—◦—

China's neighbours are unconvinced by China's ritual phrases that all countries big and small are equal or that China will never seek hegemony. 1994

—◦—

It would be imprudent not to expect a resurgent China in 50 years. Whether China will be more democratic and pluralistic or still authoritarian and one-party, is another matter. But the United States, Japan and Europe can together influence this outcome by engaging China, educating China's brightest and best students who study abroad. The thinking and perceptions of these young scholars will be a decisive factor in China's outward orientation. 1994

—◦—

To tell the world that China hasn't got the capability to cross 100 miles of water [to Taiwan] is to challenge them to do it. And I think they will respond to that challenge. Not that they will actually cross over, but they will display their capability, enough to get the other side to talk very seriously about a peaceful solution. I think that will take place by 2016. 1996

—◦—

All countries in Asia, medium and small, have this concern: will China seek to re-establish its traditional pattern of international relations of vassal states in a tributary relationship with the Middle Kingdom? Any signs of this will alarm all the countries in the region, and cause most countries to realign themselves closer to the US and Japan. 1996

The difficulty arises from America's expressed desire to make China more democratic. China resents and resists this as an interference in its domestic matters. Outside powers cannot re-fashion China into their own image. Let us not forget that even China's conquerors like the Mongols in the 13th and 14th centuries, and the Manchus in the 17th to 19th centuries, could not change Chinese culture. Instead China changed them and they were absorbed and assimilated. The language and culture of its conquerors could not overcome Chinese language and culture.   1996

———◦———

China's leaders have referred to me as an old friend. I am an older friend of Taiwan. If either one is damaged, Singapore will suffer a loss. If both are damaged, Singapore's loss will be doubled. Singapore benefits when both prosper, when both cooperate and help each other prosper.   1996

———◦———

What China will learn is that its influence in the world of tomorrow depends not only on its GDP and military strength but on other people's perceptions of the Chinese society, their admiration for things Chinese, i.e. 'soft power', the attractiveness of China's society, not 'hard power', which depends on economic and military strength. People must admire aspects of your society, hence the many foreign students now going to America, to study in their universities.   1997

———◦———

China's history of over 4,000 years was one of dynastic rulers, interspersed with anarchy, foreign conquerors, warlords and dictators. The Chinese people had never experienced a government based on counting heads instead of chopping off heads. Any evolution towards representative government would be gradual.   2000

As China develops and becomes a largely urban society, its political system must evolve to accommodate a large middle class that will be highly educated, better informed and connected with the outside world, one that expects a higher quality of life in a clean environment, and wants to have its views heard by a government that is transparent and free from corruption. 2005

—◦◦—

Most Chinese feel that their ancient civilisation has distinctive attributes and value systems that have served them well overseas. This cultural heritage has been romanticised and treasured. Some aspects of traditional culture and custom have been criticised as being no longer relevant, that they have become obstacles to progress. Traditional Chinese custom as practised by the early emigrants needs to be understood so that their descendants can judge and decide what is still valid today. Knowledge of the past will enable Chinese descendants overseas to observe how the Chinese in China are changing, adjusting and adapting their own tradition and custom. 2005

—◦◦—

Unlike other emergent countries, China wants to be China and accepted as such, not as an honorary member of the West. 2009

ON ECONOMICS
AND DEVELOPMENT

Progress, in the modern connotation of the word in all the emergent countries, means being industrialised, having the sinews of machines, having a standard of living which is not dependent upon the man working the *changkol* [hoe] but the man working the drill. My thesis is this: that if we lose, fritter away the next decade that we have and not make preparations for our take-off into the industrial age, then we may well live to regret it.   1962

———◦———

Euphemisms abound in these discussions to glide over the sensitivities of the new countries and soothe the conscience of the not-new countries. To be 'new' is to be developing but, to be 'developing' is often not to be developing. And not to be 'developed' is to be underdeveloped. And to be 'underdeveloped' is to be poor.   1966

———◦———

There is a hallmark of whether a country is developed or underdeveloped. If the people do not understand why they are poor and they believe that either you have a messiah who makes a speech or an army general with a gun, who looks efficient, military-like, business-like and that he can cure problems of poverty, unemployment and development, then I say you are underdeveloped, because it is only in an underdeveloped situation that such a thing can happen.   1966

Fortunately, we never attempted to subsidise rice or other staple foodstuffs. Those governments which have done so face grave problems, as more and more of their revenue goes into feeding more and more mouths at subsidised prices, generating overpopulation, under-education, low economic growth, massive unemployment and resulting social unrest. And this is what has happened because elected governments in several new countries have baulked at taking unpopular decisions.

1970

For Singapore only just getting industrialised, it will be disastrous if we think we can get more and more pay for less and less work. No one owes us a living. Nothing is for free.

1972

We are not blessed with oil or minerals or agricultural commodities. But we have got a strategic economic position, a sound infrastructure for industrial production, and efficient services, from repairing ships, aircraft and replenishing their oil and stores, to providing expertise in engineering and management problems, and an ever more efficient financial centre and money market. If everybody works his best and his hardest, real standards of living may not go up very much, but they will not go down.

1974

Did I ever contemplate nationalisation, socialist planning for industrialisation and economic transformation? Frankly, no. For there was precious little to nationalise, apart from office furniture and equipment, bank offices, shops, hotels, and some factories. Further, I had before me, by 1965, the salutary lessons of U Nu's Burma, Bandaranaike's Ceylon, and Sukarno's Indonesia.

1978

The statue of the founder of Singapore, Sir Stamford Raffles, still stands in the heart of the city to remind Singaporeans of his vision in 1819 of Singapore becoming, on the basis of free competition, the emporium of the East, on the route between India and China. There were then 120 people on the island. They lived by fishing. Within five years of its founding, there were 5,000 traders, British, Arabs, Chinese, Indians and others drawn in by this principle of free and equal competition, regardless of race, language or religion.   1978

To save one European job, say in textiles or shoes, you put 2, sometimes 2.5 to 3 persons out of jobs in the developing countries. And in the developed countries, the person who is out of a job has got the benefits of unemployment relief almost as good as if he were in the job. He only suffers the inconvenience or the stigma of not being at work and not having the pleasure of the company of his workmates. But in developing countries being out of a job means being hungry.   1978

What are the factors that have enabled us to overcome this recession better than most? First, prudent budgets for many years with no deficits for current expenditure, and a balance of payments in surplus, not in deficit. This makes our currency stable. We do not need to borrow vast sums of money, because we have not overspent. When we do have to spend more than we earn that year, we have savings to dig into. A reliable Singapore dollar has helped us develop our banking and financial institutions, for money seeks security without impediment to its free flow.   1983

Let us not forget that protectionism and less trade mean less growth for the developing countries. This means debt burdens cannot be discharged. Defaults may be unavoidable, with incalculable consequences for the international banking system. Even if the banks survive the upheavals, these developing countries will have to abandon all thoughts of liberalisation towards plurality and more democratic freedoms. Severe or repressive government is the other side of austere or negative economic growth.   1985

—◦—

We should encourage our small and medium enterprises to link up with MNCs [multinational corporations] from countries like Japan and Germany, to be their partners so that they can get suitable technology transfers and improve their organisational methods, but our SMEs [small to medium enterprises] will have to grow on their own steam. They will grow big only if their executives have the entrepreneurial ability plus the energy and drive. Government assistance can help but will not be decisive in making our SMEs big or successful.   1992

—◦—

By several quantitative measures, including per capita income, Singapore is now ranked among the developed countries. But the government has not celebrated because we all know only too well how dependent we are on foreign technology, foreign entrepreneurs and foreign talent. We are not in the same league as America or Japan or Germany with their knowledge-and-technology-rich human resources. At a stretch, we may be equal to Portugal or Greece or Spain.   1996

—◦—

While the western MNCs have the know-how, the Asian conglomerates have the know-who as they are conveniently plugged into the social, cultural, political and business networks in the region.   1996

Like Nehru[10], I had been influenced by the ideas of the British Fabian Society. But I soon realised that before distributing the pie I had first to bake it. So I departed from welfarism because it sapped a people's self-reliance and their desire to excel and succeed. I also abandoned the model of industrialisation through import substitution. When most of the Third World was deeply suspicious of exploitation by western MNCs, Singapore invited them in. They helped us grow, brought in technology and know-how, and raised productivity levels faster than any alternative strategy could.   2005

—◦◦—

If we cannot increase the productivity or the output of our citizens, our economy will slow down. Then Singaporeans will discover that instead of many job opportunities and rising asset values, including prices for resale HDB [Housing Development Board] flats, the reverse will happen across the board. It will be worse for most people, fewer jobs, lower salaries, lower asset prices including HDB home values and resale prices. Young Singaporeans will face more difficulties finding jobs to support themselves and their families. So although more new flats will be available, they cannot afford to buy these flats when they are not earning good incomes. Opportunities will diminish for Singapore citizens. We will have a deflating economy, with a series of knock-on effects as prices of all assets including flats will go down, demand will lessen, pay will fall and so will the number of jobs and promotions. When this happens, many of our own talents will leave for greener pastures, which will exacerbate the downward spiral and eventually lead to Singapore's decline.

2010

ON PROSPERITY

Estate duty is one of those forms of taxation which can be used deliberately to counterbalance the unjust distribution of wealth and prevent its perpetuation. The primary purpose of a socialist taxation policy is to bring about a redistribution of wealth. You take the money from the 'haves' and then you spend it on your education, on your public services, and on your social welfare, and thereby give it to the have-nots. You have this added advantage in that you really do not hurt anybody because you have really taken it from no one. All you have taken away from the sons and heirs and successors is not money, but just the hope of a succeeding to money. That might be painful for a week or two after the will has been read and duties have to be paid, but it is certainly less painful than if we were to impose a capital levy while the man who has made his millions is still alive.   1955

—◦◦—

Wealth and poverty are relative things. You have acute tensions, either within a society or internationally within an international community, not so much because you are too poor as against another person or you are too rich, in the absolute sense, but whether you are relatively too much better off than the other to cause the other fellow dissatisfaction.   1962

—◦◦—

We have been able over the last 16 years to bring about an economic and social transformation. We have made joining the communists and dying in a guerrilla revolution not an attractive alternative to learning a skill, holding a job, owning your flat with your fridge, your TV, your washing machine and raising your wife and two children.   1975

The poor know that you don't get manna falling from heaven, not in
Singapore anyway.   1976

—◦—

Today, one of our problems is that many young people believe that prosperity
and growth are part of the nature of Singapore. It is necessary to remind them
that prosperity and growth do not come naturally in a place without natural
resources. They are the result of man's effort and ingenuity.   1977

—◦—

Every citizen already feels he has a stake, a sense of proprietorship, in the
stability and progress of Singapore. Every citizen can expect to get his
commensurate shares of the prosperity to which he has contributed.   1978

—◦—

Singapore is a society based on effort and merit, not wealth and privilege
depending on birth. There is nothing in the lifestyle of the employer which
is not open to the worker. If the executives play squash, tennis or golf, so can
workers. If executives go on holidays abroad, so do workers.   1989

—◦—

It is nonsense to say that this government is rich while the people are poor.
This is true only when the leaders steal the nation's wealth. In Singapore,
leaders are not thieves, so when the government is rich, it means we the
people are rich with the money to guarantee security and benefits for all the
people.   1992

Everybody in Singapore wants to own a condominium, or a landed property. Unfortunately not everybody can get landed property. However, within 15 years, the main upgrading programme will give everybody the improvements that will totally change the present [HDB] blocks and make them like condominiums.

1996

———◇◇———

Our young should prepare to seek their fortunes in this golden age. It is silly to moan that properties and cars are going out of their reach. They will never be out of reach of those who seize their opportunities. Of course those on profit-sharing schemes and stock options will do better than those on salaries. But even those on salaries will have their salaries double in the next 10 years of high growth.

1996

———◇◇———

We cannot have everybody own a car, however high our per capita income may be: our young must accept the fact that we cannot afford to have our roads jammed up and that this will harm our economy. We cannot give everybody landed property, a terrace house or a bungalow. We do not have the land for it. But we can provide everybody with high-rise and high-quality homes, and high-quality public transport.

1996

———◇◇———

For over 30 years we have aimed for an egalitarian society. If we want to have successful entrepreneurs, Singaporeans have to accept a greater income disparity between the successful and the not so successful.

2002

We all have to accept some sacrifices and cutbacks. But compared to our counterparts in neighbouring countries, Malaysia, Thailand, Philippines, Indonesia, Myanmar, Cambodia and Vietnam, our low-income earners are much better off. We will make sure that nobody falls through the cracks and drops below the poverty line. The government has to be prudent. Everyone has to put up with some austerity until the economy turns around when the world economy picks up.

2008

⸺◦⸺

Everyone's wealth has shrunk as our assets have lost value. But if you have not borrowed excessively to buy assets and have sufficient cash to service your loans, you can hold on to your investments until the market turns up and prices recover. Singaporeans need not despair or be depressed. We will have to endure some hardship. But nobody will be destitute, depending on soup kitchens or begging in the streets. Everyone has a home, 95% of Singaporeans are homeowners.

2009

⸺◦⸺

Whatever your job, you are better off in Singapore than if you are in a similar job in any other Asian country, including China and India. The only country where job for job you can be better off, is Japan.

2009

ON ENTREPRENEURSHIP
AND INNOVATION

Let us recognise that no nation in the world ever gives away a technological advantage for reasons of charity.   1967

The aeroplane may have taken over the bulk of passenger travel. But into the foreseeable future no technological breakthrough can replace ships as the most efficient and economic form of transportation of goods. If we build up a reputation for fast work, of good quality, at fair prices, ship-repairing and shipbuilding will become one of our great industries.   1970

Knowledge and technology once disseminated, cannot be put back into the bottle and corked up.   1992

I wish you well. How well you do depends on how enterprising you are. That is what private enterprise means.   1992

We cannot predict which of our younger managers, engineers and professionals will have the entrepreneurial flair. It has to be by trial and error, tossing them into the deep end of the pool.   1993

Corporations that get their ideas from only one culture will lose out on innovations.

1995

There is a glorious rainbow that beckons those with the spirit of adventure. And there are rich findings at the end of that rainbow. To the young and the not too old, I say look at the horizon, find that rainbow, go ride it. Not all will be rich; quite a few will find a vein of gold; but all who pursue that rainbow will have a joyous and exhilarating ride and some profit.

1996

Hong Kongers are better prepared than Singaporeans for this next phase because they have always been risk-takers. By history, our young have always taken the safer course of joining a big corporation, usually an MNC [multinational corporation] or local corporations, and climbing up within their ranks. Hong Kongers, after joining a company, leave as soon as they have learned the ropes to start up their own, betting their last shirt on their venture in order to hit that jackpot. Not everybody has got the inventiveness and shrewdness to go for such ventures. We must encourage and support those who have. We must help them spawn many new small enterprises, some of which will grow big.

2000

The key to innovation and technology is people. We must develop and nurture our talent so that innovation and creativity will be integral to education and training. Our education system is being revamped to nurture innovation and creativity, from kindergarten to university, and on to lifelong learning. Equally important, we will tap foreign talent, by making Singapore a more attractive place to live in.

2000

The dream of wealth attracts everyone. But it is those who innovate in creating new products or services, who will be the new rich. Few are born entrepreneurs, and not many will succeed. To succeed as an entrepreneur one has to have some extraordinary qualities such as high energy levels, a cut of mind that sees opportunities where others see problems, and a keen sense of what product or service will be profitable.   2002

Japanese people have been excellent in perfecting technologies. The standard example was the way they improved on the Chinese abacus which has seven beads, two above, five below, rounded and noisy. The Japanese reduced the seven beads to five, one above, four below, with sharp edges, silent and fast. So too Japanese chopsticks. The pointed ends make it easier to manage small rounded morsels like peanuts that are difficult to handle with the Chinese chopsticks. This ability to improve on present technology is worth preserving and maintaining. But improving on what others have invented is not enough. You have to be like the Americans and invent products that others have not thought of, that will be desired and bought by billions across the world.   2003

No nation has ever become the major power without a clear lead in technology, both civilian and military. From the Roman legions, to the naval powers of Portugal, Spain and Great Britain, to Germany in World War I and the US post-World War II, great power status was achieved by those nations that were able to harness their technological advantage for holistic development of their civilian and military capabilities.   2005

ON THE WORKPLACE

I know that change is sometimes unpleasant, particularly when, if you have been working at a leisurely pace and somebody comes along to put the heat on you.

1967

—◦◦◦—

The assumptions made in the 1950s and 1960s by the trade unions and their advisers, of whom I was one, were that our workers wanted more leisure to enjoy their pay. These assumptions were based on British practices which were and are completely irrelevant to our social conditions. Everybody knows this. Our workers want work, and more work for more money – not more leisure to spend the inadequate sums they earn.

1968

—◦◦◦—

In the earlier stages of our labour movement, the trade union often became a place of refuge for the inefficient, the slack, the lazy and the anti-social. As has happened elsewhere, these are the first to join the union to seek protection against the natural desire of any employer to be rid of bad workers. [...] I am not asking our trade union leaders, in an open democratic society, to take on the role of management. But I do urge them, with the help of these new laws, to stop giving cover to those who do not pull their weight. We must avoid slipping into a situation where trade unionism is the practice of protecting the weakest and the slowest worker and, with everybody being paid the same wage, nobody will have the slightest incentive to work harder than the weakest and the slowest.

1968

—◦◦◦—

Just as there are bad workers, so too there are bad employers. [...] These employers will have to be educated and taught the facts of present-day industrial life.

1968

Employers must understand that good personnel relations are an asset. If you have supervisors who are rude and crude to Singaporeans, our self-respect demands that we put a stop to this. We can make our workers strive harder. But we will not allow them to be humiliated or browbeaten.   1970

———◦———

You can bargain for better wages, you can bargain for higher productivity bonuses. But once the bargain has been struck, then you must enter into the spirit of the agreement, and put in an honest day's work for an honest day's wage. There must be no fooling around, work means discipline. Singapore's success depends on the spirit in which workers, management and government, all three, enter into the spirit of cooperation, necessary for prosperity.   1970

———◦———

One good management team gives 10,000 men their jobs.   1975

———◦———

There are jobs that must be done. And whether they are in air-conditioned offices or factories or out in the sun and rain, the work has to be done, and done well. That is our way forward.   1976

———◦———

A skilled [Japanese] worker will clean up his machine and polish up the floor around it, whilst the Singaporean expects the floor to be cleaned by somebody else because it is not his duty. The Singaporean's attention is confined to his own job and his promotion prospects. He is not keen to widen his responsibilities. That together he and his fellow workers can make the company more efficient and productive, and therefore make more profits, bringing more wages for everyone – this is too vague a vision and does not move him. Too many workers have not identified themselves with their companies like the Japanese workers do.   1976

The Singapore worker is intelligent and quick to learn. But the Singaporean soon believes that he has learnt all there is to learn, when in fact he has not reached the standards of the Japanese skilled worker or technician.   1976

—◦◦—

We do not have antagonistic relations between workers and managers. There are no conflicts between those who feel, or are made to feel, that they are exploited; and those who are, or are made out to be, on the side of the exploiters. Had we allowed ourselves to be trapped in these simplistic concepts of the Marxist class struggle, Singapore would have been ruined.   1978

—◦◦—

For Singapore, the 1960s was the decade when unemployment was solved; the 1970s was the decade of near-full employment and acquisition of simple skills; the 1980s must be a decade of maturity as our workers seek to perfect their skills and raise their productivity. The progress of the last 20 years was made possible because of the close, almost inseparable, ties between the leaders of the PAP and the NTUC [National Trade Union Congress]. In fact, they are one leadership: a group of men had launched a movement to oust the British; they ran into and surmounted communist dominance in mass organisation; the leadership which emerged was balanced and stable.   1979

—◦◦—

We are a multiracial, immigrant society of willing and quick learners. Unfortunately most of us expect quick results and quicker returns. The Singaporean places great emphasis on certificates, on his legal rights and obligations. There is no great pride in the job, nor that self-esteem which makes a German or a Japanese excel in whatever he has to do.   1979

A Japanese doctor or a Korean computer system analyst will think twice before emigrating to America, Canada, Australia or New Zealand. He has major adjustments to make, linguistically and culturally. The English-educated Singaporean is completely at home in the English language, and his cultural adjustments are minimal compared to the trauma a Japanese or Korean will suffer. This poses special dangers for us. Unless we can provide our able graduates a satisfying career in Singapore, one where rewards, job satisfaction, and the prospects for their children's education and future are comparable to those which they can slowly, but painstakingly, create for themselves if they settle in the US, Canada, Australia or New Zealand as minority Asians, we shall be depleted of talent. 1982

One crucial lesson I have learnt is that militant, powerful, antagonistic trade unions who set out to confront employers in order to extract the maximum for their members, regardless of the interests of the employers or workers in other sectors, end up by successfully scuttling the whole of their own economy and demolishing their own societies. Look at Britain and Australia. Singapore unions and leaders, including myself, were once as bloody-minded. In our first phase, we were fiercely anti-colonial and anti-capitalist. We wanted to get rid of the British and their big business houses, to get independence and power into our own hands. We wanted to cut the cake up our way, with larger pieces for our workers. Fortunately, we learnt the hard facts of life quickly. From 1959, with self-government, and especially from 1965, with independence, alone on our own, we realised that we needed to create stable secure conditions for investment, with favourable prospects for profitable returns. Otherwise the economy would not have moved and unemployment would have become crippling. 1983

The Japanese worker can be a model. A Japanese waiter is proud to be an excellent waiter and goes about his work efficiently, with grace and style. A Japanese cook is proud of his excellent training. When he appears at your table in a hotel or restaurant to present his dishes, he is clean, smart and cheerful, and he slices the sashimi or fruit and serves his guests with panache. So also Japanese salesmen and managers. These are the people I come into contact with when I visit Japan. The other side of 'excellence' is 'average' or 'mediocre'. The Japanese have their average, but their average is of very high standards.   1987

———◦◦———

Fighting the boss successfully does not necessarily bring good to the workers. Indeed by defeating the boss, the workers will succeed in defeating the company and destroying their jobs. Instead, Japanese unions have shown that cooperating with intelligent management to achieve high productivity brings pay increases and job security.   1989

———◦◦———

The quality of a nation's manpower resources is the single most important factor determining national competitiveness. It is a people's innovativeness, entrepreneurship, teamwork and their work ethic that give them that sharp keen edge in competitiveness.   1990

———◦◦———

Troublesome employers will soon run into trouble with their profits, because if they don't get the cooperation of their workers, their competitor who does get the cooperation of his workers will beat them.   1995

The things we do today our neighbours will be able to do at lower cost in five or more years. We must move on to more complex work using more complex machines and computers, always keeping ahead in our education.   1999

—◦—

To get employed, old workers must adjust their wage expectations, their lifestyle and take less comfortable jobs. Even those previously working in the manufacturing industry need further training to acquire new skills needed for the new jobs whether in industry or services. Such economic restructuring is inevitable because jobs and industries become redundant, and the new industries that emerge require new skills.   2003

ON THE WELFARE STATE

There is nothing wrong about free health and education, if a society can afford it. But a developing country which wants to develop, cannot afford a large increase in population. There should be more than token payments for use of these services if the ills consequent on too rapid a population growth are to be avoided. Parents must know the costs of these services. Beyond the third child, fiscal policies must be devised to check the irresponsible from putting the costs of bringing up their children on the backs of the hard-working and economically productive, who already pay more than their fair share of taxes and, because they have small families, use less than their share of these services.

1970

We are mindful of the dangers of high welfare and unemployment benefits, watching the consequences of this compassionate policy on the job-seeking habits of the unemployed. Visiting the major cities of the industrial countries, I am struck by this curious phenomena of high unemployment and yet a shortage of waiters, cab drivers, nurses and garbage collectors. Some jobs are not worth doing, as a result of welfare benefits. Whatever principles may be applicable in highly developed industrial countries, for a resource-poor country like Singapore, hard work, and high performance amply rewarded, is the best way to attract capital and technology into the country to generate wealth.

1978

When people get equal handouts, whether or not they work harder or better, everybody then works less hard. The country must go down. It is when people are encouraged to excel by being able to keep a large part of the extra reward earned by their extra efforts that the society as a whole becomes wealthier and everyone thrives and prospers.

1984

We have used to advantage what Britain left behind: the English language, the legal system, parliamentary government and impartial administration. However, we have studiously avoided the practices of the welfare state. We saw how a great people reduced themselves to mediocrity by levelling down. The less enterprising and less hardworking cannot be made equal simply by cutting down the achievements of the enterprising and the striving. And we have seen how difficult it is to dismantle a system of subsidised living once people get accustomed to a government providing for them.   1985

—◦—

Do we need to learn all over again when we can see what happened to the British and the Australians? They went in for compassionate welfare programmes. They paid their unemployed almost as much as the employed when they lost their jobs. They had the right to refuse three or four jobs until the right one came along, commensurate with what he was getting the last time, to his liking. The result was the layabouts.   · 1989

—◦—

I have a theory which explains why resource-rich countries like Australia and Canada are different. They are large continents with small populations that will not be able to consume their cornucopia of national resources, not in a thousand years. This immense wealth has created the resource-rich syndrome. This syndrome results in a relaxed not intense society. Such a society lacks the motivation for high performances, because of the high social security and welfare their governments can afford. Through subsidies, price supports and welfare payments they spread the wealth equally around with little or no effort from the people. Hence Australians and Canadians and to a small extent New Zealanders have had high consumption, low savings, low competitiveness, high current account deficit and high debt.   1994

I will be very unhappy if I went around Singapore and in spite of our prosperity, I saw a few hundred people living on the streets, begging, playing a violin, or pretending to play a violin to collect money. That means something has gone wrong with the society. They have not been given the proper chance.

1995

—◦◦—

First, we give everyone basic health care. Second, we have different grades of health care for those who want more than the basic. We have achieved what is fair health care for everybody, not equal health care, but fair and practical. We are not equal, we do not eat equal food, how can we demand equal medicine? We often get demagogues who come up and say this is exploitation of the poor, that they will give the best doctors and the best surgeons for the poor etc. They may get some votes, but most people do not believe that is practical and do not believe them.

1995

—◦◦—

I read a *Straits Times* poll that 9 out of 10 of those surveyed felt that it was the government's job to help the poor and that nearly half felt that the government was not doing enough. This is the easiest way to destroy self-reliance which has been a driving force for high performance. Many Singaporeans feel that the government can afford it. This is precisely the trap which the advanced countries fell into when economic growth was robust and compassion was believed to be always affordable.

1996

More can and will be done for the elderly, the young and the needy, provided we can find the men and women to give their time. The government will provide the buildings and facilities. What the government cannot provide is the personal touch and the direct contact of voluntary social workers. Their altruistic and charitable feelings can motivate people to help themselves. Many welfare schemes in the West become bureaucratic and wasteful, because paid officials do not have those feelings and sentiments of altruism and idealism which volunteer social workers have. Hence paid officials cannot generate reciprocal feelings of appreciation and gratitude from those they help. It is this crucial factor of high morale, both in the giver and in the receiver, that makes the difference between the communitarian way of welfare which is effective, as against official or bureaucratic welfare which demotivates those receiving handouts.   1997

Welfare and subsidies destroy the motivation to perform and succeed. Where we must help, give cash or assets and leave it to the individual to decide how he will spend it. When people become dependent on subsidies, and the government can no longer afford and has to cut subsidies, people riot.   2006

ON LIFE

There are some countries in the world which make solemn undertakings and immediately and frivolously disavow them. In the end nobody believes them. Their promises become worthless.

1963

⸺◦⸺

As you solve a set of problems, new ones appear. That is part of the nature of life.

1968

⸺◦⸺

If there is one touchstone for success, it is confidence. A people must have confidence in themselves. If they lack it, if they feel they are unequal to the challenge, then they will never make the grade.

1968

⸺◦⸺

I believe the human being wants an equal chance with his fellow human being, regardless of his father's wealth or status in order that he can do his best, in order that he can compete and climb up to the top. And that is so, whether you are in Moscow, whether you are in Peking, whether you are in Washington or London. And you can't reverse human nature.

1976

⸺◦⸺

I believe that life is a process of continuous change and a constant struggle to make that change one for the better.

1978

Every generation has a quota of those who feel that society does not give them the status, the position, the influence, the rewards, that they deserve. They want to overturn the order of things. 1987

———◦◦◦———

Even in the capitalist West where they have tried throwing money at problems, what is the end result? You go down New York, Broadway. You will see the beggars, people on the streets. Worse than in the 1950s and in the early '60s before the Great Society programmes. Why? Why did it get worse after compassion moved a President, motivated with a great vision of a society which was wealthy and cared for, could look after everybody – the blacks, the minorities, the dispossessed, the disadvantaged. There is more unhappiness and more hardship today and more beggars, more muggers. Why is that? Have we not learnt? Where are the beggars in Singapore? Show me. I take pride in that. Has anybody died of starvation? Anybody without a home left to die in the streets and have to be collected as dead corpses? Because we came to the realistic conclusion that the human being is motivated by instincts that go deep down into the basic genes of life. And the first basic instinct is to protect yourself, and stronger than that, to protect your offspring so that there is the next generation. You kill that link, you have killed off mankind. 1989

———◦◦◦———

Loyalty is not something that can be measured quantitatively like height or weight. It is in the mind, in the heart. It is a question of our gut feelings. 2001

———◦◦◦———

I believe you are what you are and very often, there's very little that polishing can do to make you different. 2003

ON ASIAN VALUES

Whilst we admire and must learn and acquire their science and technology, their management skills and marketing know-how, we do not seek to model our lives on Western social mores and their contemporary lifestyles. We must learn the experience of the Japanese – how, in less than a hundred years since the Meiji Restoration of 1868, they have become a modern industrial state, without abandoning their own cultural traditions.   1977

———◦———

We must not allow our values and our philosophy of what is good government to be overwhelmed by the standards and norms of the contemporary West, regardless of their relevance to our social, economic and political conditions, simply because, for the time being the West have the material abundance and technological superiority. Let us select the relevant factors in their societies, factors which have made them strong and have been proven by the test of time. Then we can incorporate these factors into our system without damage to ourselves.   1977

———◦———

We have developed and progressed not because we were a Western-Occidental-type society, but because we were an Asian-Oriental-type society, hardworking, thrifty and disciplined, a people with Asian values, strong family ties and responsibility for the extended family which is a common feature of Asian cultures, whether Chinese, Malay or Indian.   1978

With the widespread use of English, TV, the cinema, magazines, books and tourists, Western values, culture and attitudes to life have permeated our society, particularly the young. We cannot isolate ourselves from the changing moods and thoughts of the world and the no-marriage family relationships Americans and some Europeans are experimenting with. But we can inoculate ourselves from the fashionable but passing fads and fancies. We can do this by retaining the core of our own basic cultural values, a keen sense of our own identity, our different inheritance and history and the self-confidence this awareness gives. Therefore, we must continue the study of our mother tongues.   1978

What is good government? This depends on the values of a people. What Asians value may not be what Americans or Europeans value. Westerners value the freedoms and liberties of the individual. As an Asian of Chinese cultural background, my values are for a government which is honest, effective and efficient in protecting its people and allowing opportunities for all to advance themselves in a stable and orderly society where they can live a good life and raise their children to do better than themselves.   1992

Asia is no Ali Baba cave of riches. East Asia is resource-poor. These countries are becoming richer by depending on their peoples' hard work, thrift, high savings, low consumption and high investments. They are intense people by culture. They are especially geared for scholarship and high performances. It is to make up for their poor resources that they have developed into intense cultures with habits of thrift and hard work.   1994

East Asians are highly competitive peoples training themselves to win life's marathons.   1994

My experience in governing Singapore, especially the difficult early years from 1959 to 1969, convinced me that we would not have surmounted our difficulties and setbacks if a large part of the population of Singapore were not imbued with Confucian values. The people had a group cohesion and a pragmatic approach to government and to the problems in society. Confucianist traditions have made Chinese Singaporeans revere scholarship and academic excellence, and also respect officials when they are chosen on the basis of their scholarship.   1994

—◦◦—

Seventy-six per cent of Singapore's population were Chinese whose culture placed great store on the *Wu Lun* or Five Relationships: between father and son, there should be affection; between Sovereign and Minister, righteousness; between husband and wife, attention to their separate functions; between old and young, a proper order; and between friends, fidelity. They accepted that the interests of society were above that of the individual. They did not believe in the unlimited individualism of the Americans.   1994

—◦◦—

A point worth noting is that most Chinese Singaporeans are descendants of immigrants, mostly poor and uneducated. They were not scholars or intellectuals who, as a result of the May Fourth Movement, rejected Confucianism. The people at large had no formal instruction in Confucianism, i.e. high culture, but practised Confucian precepts in their daily lives. What they had was the low culture or folk culture, based on practices learnt from parents and relatives, encapsulated in proverbs and sayings based on Confucianism, Taoism and Buddhism.   1994

—◦◦—

I think the Americans seem to be willing to spend now and to mortgage the future, whereas no society in East Asia is mortgaging its future and letting their children pay for it. They are saving up to give their children a better start.   1995

As a person of Chinese background, I have values which are different from Americans or the Westerners. If you ask them they will say that democracy, freedom, human rights, all the constitutional guarantees of rights and freedom of the individual are the most important. I visited America, I am puzzled, sometimes alarmed, at the lawlessness, rampant crime, muggings, drug-taking, use of guns, violence and large number of homeless on the streets. I feel it's a dangerous place. You have to know which places you can go to and which places to avoid. It is a polarized society, very wealthy suburbs, wealthy areas, and the slums. It is not an Asian's idea of an ideal society. My idea of a good society is one where everybody has enough to eat, a home, good health, good education for their children and a good future for them. To do that, we must have a strong, clean government, which is fair, which is honest, which works to provide people with equal opportunities, regardless of their race, religion and sex. So, everybody can make his best contribution and get the maximum return for his contribution.

1995

———◦◦◦———

Clan groups should keep abreast with a fast changing world. A *hui guan*[11] should not be merely a place to play mahjong.

1997

———◦◦◦———

One fundamental difference between American and Oriental culture is the individual's position in society. In American culture an individual's interest is primary. This makes American society more aggressively competitive, with a sharper edge and higher performance. In Singapore, the interests of the society take precedence over that of the individual. Nevertheless Singapore has to be competitive in the market for jobs, goods and services. On the other hand the government helps lower income groups to meet their needs for housing, health services and education so that their children will have more of an equal chance to rise through education.

2004

ON THE FAMILY

The object of any organised society is the pursuit of the happiness and the well-being of all its peoples. My opinion is that, in our pursuit of this happiness, we should do something to alleviate the sufferings and hardships of those who wish to avoid unduly large families by having the assistance of family planning.   1955

—◦◦◦—

Quite apart from religious principles, by and large, Chinese and Indian families believe that the more children a man has the greater is his good fortune. In the old days the more wives a man had, the higher his status. Just like motor cars, wives and children were a status symbol. All this proliferating made sense in an age when periodic plagues, drought, floods and famine regularly decimated the population. But the same habits in a relatively affluent society, whose public health standards are high, lead to a phenomenal increase in population growth that cannot but dampen the spirits of those who are entrusted with our problems of economic growth, industrial expansion and the maintenance of standards of living.   1963

—◦◦◦—

One of the noticeable trends in developed countries is that parents with more education have much smaller families than those with less education. This trend is also discernible in urbanised, though still underdeveloped, societies like Singapore. If these trends continue to their logical conclusions, then the quality of the population will go down. In all societies, there are the more intelligent and the less intelligent. [Some] geneticists have come to the conclusion that intelligence is principally determined by heredity. It is not unlikely that many other attributes of mind and body are also inherited. But whatever the inheritance, man, more than any other living creature, depends on nurturing and training for his capacity to mature and to develop.   1969

When the less educated who are also in the lower income groups have large families, the problems they create for their children are compounded. Resources, time, attention and care, lavished on one or two children, can nurture and develop the endowments of the children to their fullest extent; when spread and frittered over six or more in the family, [they] prevent any child from getting the chances he could have had in a smaller family. In urbanised Singapore, this can become an acute problem.   1969

———◦◦———

There are certain areas of activity over which control by any government is both difficult and repugnant. One such area is the choice of the number of children a father and mother decide to rear. One day the pressure of circumstances may become so acute that attitudes must change. Until such time when moral inhibitions disappear and legislative or administrative measures can be taken to regulate the size of families, we must try to induce people to limit their families and give their children a better chance.   1969

———◦◦———

Every person, genius or moron, has a right to reproduce himself. So we assume that a married pair will want to be allowed two children to replace them. This is already the average size family of the skilled industrial worker in Europe. In Singapore we still allow three for good measure. Beyond the three children, the costs of subsidised housing, socialised medicine and free education should be transferred to the parent.   1969

———◦◦———

With a lower birthrate, we can reach out for higher goals. We can achieve a better standard of living and a higher quality of life. With smaller families, we can invest more in each child, better health, education and training, and higher performance.   1972

I hope we can avoid most of the problems that have troubled Western societies, of too many unmarried mothers and high rates of divorce, as the use of the pill became widespread. And we must, by income tax and Housing Board concessions for those with retired parents living with them, try to sustain the Asian tradition of caring for the old within the family, instead of sending them into state or welfare institutions, where the occasional family visit is the last vestige of filial obligation. 1975

———◦◦◦———

The first principle of any civilisation is orderly living and the rearing of the young. 1977

———◦◦◦———

Today, there are more divorces than there were ten years ago and remarriages and broken marriages. It's all the sign of change for the worst. [...] And I am not sure at all that what I am seeing, experimenting with lifestyles [...] Mr., Mrs., Miss – now they have Ms. What does that mean? That means belongs to nobody? I don't know. I think this is a curious world, this is a twilight world. Let's go slow, let's not change in this. 1978

———◦◦◦———

Traditional beliefs die hard. In the year of the dragon (1976), Chinese births went up by 9.8% from 30,635 the year before (rabbit), to 33,627. For 1977 (serpent), Chinese births went down by 11.5% to 29,758. Such are the curious results when old beliefs find expression through modern biological controls of fertility. Government planners will have to take these preferences into account to interpret trends, and to anticipate demands for hospital services, schools and universities. Further, the Ministry of Defence will have to make adjustments for their manpower intake, depending on the animal year it was 18 years ago! 1978

There is one aspect of this process of change or modernisation which we must avoid at all costs – that is the break up of the three-generation family. The three-generation family is a rarity now in Western Europe and in America. Yet it is still common in Japan, South Korea, Taiwan and Hong Kong, despite their industrialisation and modernisation. It is a question of family structure, of social framework, of filial ties and bonds, which hold family units together. Our strong family structure has been a great strength for continuity in bringing up our next generation. The family has transmitted social values, more by osmosis than by formal instruction. We must preserve this precious family structure if our society is to regenerate itself without loss of cultural vigour, compassion and wisdom. There is another compelling reason why we must preserve the three-generation family: simply, that we do not have the land to build the flats needed if we break up the three-generation family.   1982

———◦———

This is a highly competitive world. We survive by being competitive. If we don't do the internet better than our neighbours, we'll be out of business. But if we allow it to make our people permissive, promiscuous, relaxed and it unravels the family and the extended family, then I say we are undone and finished, because family strength and social cohesion were the basis on which we built Singapore.   1996

———◦———

We cannot measure our happiness just by our GDP growth. It is how our families and friends care for each other, how we look after our old and nurture our young, they are what make for a closely knit society, one we can be proud to belong to.   1997

To reproduce ourselves each woman must have 2.1 children. Immigration can make up the loss but natural replacement is better. Our educated should have three children per family. In this way we can keep strong that core of native-born Singaporeans. They will keep Singapore going through thick and thin and never give up, however difficult the problems. 2001

———◦———

If in fact it is true, and I have asked doctors this, that you are genetically born a homosexual – because that's the nature of the genetic random transmission of genes – you can't help it. So why should we criminalise it? 2007

ON THE GENERATIONS

The past generations were divided according to the countries from which they emigrated to Malaya. The present generation are sometimes finding it not very easy to come together because of the different languages they learnt in different schools, none of which taught them a common language. Let us bring up our children, the future generation, to be proud of their cultural traditions and heritage, but prouder still of the new nation that we are now forging out of the different races who have come to settle and build up the Malaya that we know today.   1961

In a society where the old maps and old compass are no longer valid and the people are on the march and on the move, at that particular moment in history it is the younger people who assume leadership.   1961

A new generation is growing up, more united, better educated and emotionally and psychologically prepared and equipped to meet the challenge of their time. You can see them in the schools. You can see them in the younger students at our universities. You can see them in our completely multiracial National Service training centres. They are a different breed, self-reliant, bouncing with confidence, eager to learn, willing to work. They expect nothing for free. And there will be leaders amongst them able and strong enough to take the torch from us and to carry it forward to light up their future.   1968

That we have the will, the ability and the discipline with which to acquire higher knowledge and new skills, there is little doubt. The question is whether the next generation will have the same drive to keep well out in front fighting against the complacency which greater comfort and ease bring in their train.

1970

———◇———

Our young are ambitious and energetic. They must also acquire those qualities which enabled their parents to make Singapore what it is today – the grit and determination to stay the course, the strength and stamina to ride over rough patches.

1974

———◇———

We are in the final stage of this transition to a next generation of leaders. By this time next year, the majority in Parliament and in the Cabinet will be the younger generation. I am like the conductor of an orchestra whose star players and supporting musicians have changed. They must play as well so that the music is as full and resonant as when the old stars were the leading players.

1984

———◇———

Younger Singaporeans are better educated. They have more knowledge, though that does not make them wiser. But being better educated, they can easily gain information; they are able to read and acquire information in newspapers, magazines, radio, television and through travel. They want more consultation and participation in the major decisions which affect their lives. I believe this is a sign of growing maturity. It is a change which can be positive. For Singapore can only be defended if Singaporeans accept the responsibility for its defence through National Service. For Singapore can only prosper if there is widespread support for, and participation in, the implementation of the policies of the government.

1984

If we can distil the essence of the experience and conclusions of the older and transmit them to the younger generation, how fortunate we would not be? If the human mind were like computers, how marvellous it would be. The quintessence of one generation's experience could be extracted and fed from one brain to another. Alas, the brain works differently. 1984

—◦—

In the middle 1980s we noticed a change in young people. They appeared less Confucian and placed more emphasis on individual rights and the freedom to 'do their own thing'. Rapid development and growth had increased incomes and increased exposure to Western media, and Western tourists. Many families travelled on holidays abroad. They were not as traditional in their values and attitudes as their elder brothers of 10–20 years ago. So we decided to reinforce family influence with formal lessons in schools to teach Confucian ethics and the different religions. The objective is to restrict the Westernisation of Singapore society. Unfortunately, this led to an outburst of Christian missionary zeal, seeking conversions. This provoked a reaction from Buddhists and Muslims who also increased their missionary fervour. So we had to stop all formal teaching of Confucianism and religions. We now only teach civics and good citizenship from Primary One to Secondary Four i.e. age six to age 16. 1994

—◦—

I'm of a different generation. I'm not interested in changing either my suit or my car or whatever with every change in fashion. That's irrelevant. I don't judge myself or my friends by their fashions. Of course, I don't approve of people who are sloppy and unnecessarily shabby or dishevelled. You don't have to be like that. But I'm not impressed by a $5,000 or $10,000 Armani suit. 1995

The regional and international setting has never been more favourable in East Asia. So I am amazed that some young Singaporeans believe that their future will be harder than their parents'. They simply do not know what a difficult and dangerous world their parents lived in, how unpromising Southeast Asia was in the 1950s to the 1970s, wracked by riots and revolution, and how much better off they are now. They are too concerned about the rising property prices.   1996

———◇———

You are better placed than your fathers: better educated, able to use English and your mother tongue. Singapore is now a brand name for integrity, efficiency, transparency, consistency and resourcefulness. But what my generation has is that fire in the belly. We knew war and enemy occupation. We have experienced fear, hunger and hardship, the terrors of communist insurgency, of communal riots and bloodshed. These trials and tribulations have steeled us for life.   2004

ON EDUCATION

It is essential for an institution of higher learning that there should be absolute academic freedom. This includes the freedom to discuss any political subject and to adopt any political attitude, within the confines of that academic institution.   1955

—◦—

In the underdeveloped regions of the world newly emerged, if somewhat prematurely, to independence, we have to make up for lost time. For in the pre-independence phase of all the colonial universities, be they British, French, Dutch, Belgian or otherwise, they only teach you the bare minimum to make you reasonably competent assistants.   1960

—◦—

If I have to choose one profession in which you give the most for the least it is probably teaching – if you take it seriously. You have to have the temperament for it to coax, to stimulate, to cajole, to discipline a young mind into good habits. You must have an aptitude.   1966

—◦—

At the end of the day, when you have left your school and you felt that you had left a friend and mentor behind, then that man whom you felt so much for and who must have felt for you to have given of himself, that man deserves a gold medal. He probably will not get it because very few people will know that he deserves that gold medal and the people who know are often unimportant people.   1966

In the long run, it is the quality of our youths that will determine our future. And we have to invest in them more than any other sector. Changes are taking place in the schools. The emphasis is now on content and quality. We want our schools to produce citizens who are healthy and hardy, with a sense of social purpose and group discipline, prepared to work and to pay for what they want, never expecting something for nothing. Our schools will train students in the classrooms, in the playing fields to make them healthy and robust. But even more important, they will teach our students high standards of personal behaviour, social norms of good and bad, right and wrong. Without these values, a literate generation may be more dangerous than a completely uneducated one.   1967

We have given every student, regardless of language, race or religion, equal opportunities for education and employment. Hundreds get scholarships every year, over 150 to go to universities abroad. All are judged and rewarded according to their performance, not their fathers' wealth or status. Economic progress has resulted from this and made life better for all. This has checked communist subversion and recruitment, especially of good cadres.   1976

Performance in examinations depends upon two factors: nature and nurture – nature being the natural intelligence of the child, nurture being the training and education. Or to use computer language, it depends on hardware and software, the hardware is the size or capacity of the computer, and the software is the teaching or educational programme. What weightings are allotted to hardware as against software, or nature against nurture, is a matter of deep controversy between the experts, the psychologists and doctors. The fact is, individuals are born with different capacities. What we must set out to do, therefore, is to help students achieve the maximum potential of whatever nature has endowed them with. In other words, to nurture them, to give them the software, to encourage, support and help them to achieve their fullest.

1982

A person learns most vividly and remembers longest and best when his lessons are accompanied by sharp pain or great joy. After he has enjoyed his first encounter with the durian, he will never forget how to identify the fragrance. Some can learn by watching others scald themselves. Few or none can learn to sniff out a good durian without having eaten both good and bad ones.

1984

———⊸∘⊶———

All over the world, every community depends on its most successful to give a boost and a helping hand to the less successful. One of the reasons for the level of education in the Chinese community is that from colonial days successful Chinese have built schools and a university to improve the lot of the less successful.

1990

———⊸∘⊶———

The key to our success in the next lap is a better educated and trained people. This is one area where we should have done better. If Singapore did not have the difficult problem of the mother tongue and English, we would have achieved some 10 to 15 years ago, what we have only now been able to do, namely get 15 to 16 per cent of each year's cohort to university and another 25 to 30 per cent to the polytechnics.

1992

———⊸∘⊶———

Your father may be a coolie or a professional, but you can reach the highest positions in government if you are an outstanding scholar.

1994

———⊸∘⊶———

East Asian students start on mathematics and sciences early in life. Effort and homework are part of growing up. Elementary-school students in Hong Kong do up to three hours of homework a day. In contrast, secondary-school students in the US and in Britain spend about five or six hours a week on homework.

1996

If your option was, I want a condo, I want a Mercedes, then you aim for those professions which will bring you those results. But you have chosen English Literature. If you were my daughter – or my granddaughter really now because my granddaughter is already 15 – I would tell her (and she also likes writing and she's in this tutor programme and she writes little stories) there's no money in it unless you are really good.   1996

———⚬———

In the '60s and '70s, we concentrated on the high-fliers, sending them to the best universities abroad, to lead our teams when they return. What we now need to do is to increase the competence of our people at every level, so that they become stronger teams for our enterprises to produce goods and services that can compete in world markets. They must be able to keep learning and retraining throughout their working lives, to stay on the right side of the global divide between those with relevant knowledge and skills, and those without.   2000

———⚬———

Imparting knowledge to pass examinations and later to do a job, these are important. However, the litmus test of a good education is whether it nurtures citizens who can live, work, contend and cooperate in a civilised way. Is he loyal and patriotic? Is he, when the need arises, a good soldier, ready to defend his country, and so protect his wife and children, and his fellow citizens?   2007

ON DISCIPLINE

If you are good, or your son is good, he will pass from primary to secondary school to university, all on scholarships; he will go abroad, come back and then the world is open to him. No other place in the world gives you this, and it is to protect and save you that whenever anybody gets out of line, we firmly take the rod and say, 'Stop, back into position'.   1967

If we want high morale, we must have high standards. If we want high standards, the law must be enforced fairly and firmly. There will be no squatters or beggars sleeping on our pavements doing their ablutions in our drains. People will be housed and cared for. Hawkers will not clog up the main streets. There will be thorough and proper cleansing every day of the year. Laws will have to be passed to help rid us of the malpractices that have crept into our workforce. Only a year before last, malingering and shirking and sabotage to create overtime and treble pay for public holidays was a way of life. Discipline and efficiency must be re-established.   1968

Quite a number of countries, after gaining independence, have failed economically and collapsed socially. They lacked one essential quality: self-discipline, either in their leaders, or more often both in their leaders and their people. It requires self-discipline to budget and live within your means, when you can just print more money. It requires self-discipline to maintain the integrity and efficiency of government and administration and to punish and keep down corruption, especially in high places.   1968

When morale is down people become apologetic and the place is in a shambles. Singapore will not be allowed to go thus. We will keep it trim, clean and green. Flowers will bloom and ferns will grow where there was dirt and tarmac. Other governments can give you fountains or stadiums or monuments. But they can't give you the capacity to organise and discipline yourselves.   1968

———

Success will depend upon getting our workers better educated with better work attitudes and more team spirit. [...] Every worker must also learn the right attitudes to work, which include a willingness to do one's work well, to be punctual, to keep one's workplace clean and tidy, and help out in the work of one's fellow-workers and to take up other side duties willingly and promptly.   1981

———

In criminal law legislation, our priority is the security and well-being of law-abiding citizens rather than the rights of the criminal to be protected from incriminating evidence.   1990

———

It is Asian values that have enabled Singapore to contain its drug problem. To protect the community we have passed laws which entitle police, drug enforcement or immigration officers to have the urine of any person who behaves in a suspicious way tested for drugs. If the result is positive, treatment is compulsory. Such a law in the United States will be unconstitutional, because it will be an invasion of privacy of the individual.   1992

———

The discipline necessary for growth has made for an orderly society with low crime rates and no major problems with drugs, large-scale illegal gambling and secret societies or mafia.   1994

As for caning, I'll give you a simple change we had to make. An illegal immigrant did not have to be caned. He was just sent to prison and fined. We found that prison was paradise compared to what he came from and the jails were being filled up. We caned. It hasn't completely deterred although it has reduced the illegals because even the caning plus the prison sentence is worth their trying to get Singapore wages. We are not punishing because we are sadists or masochists. It gives us no pleasure, but it's the only practical punishment that works; but unfortunately not as effectively as whipping would do.   1995

—◦—

I have never understood why Western educationists are so much against corporal punishment. It did my fellow students and me no harm.   1998

—◦—

I have never believed those who advocate a soft approach to crime and punishment, claiming that punishment does not reduce crime. That was not my experience in Singapore before the war, during the Japanese occupation or subsequently.   1998

—◦—

Gambling pathology, like AIDS or SARS or Avian flu, cannot be prevented from affecting Singaporeans. We can take measures to keep Singapore clean and safe, despite these dangerous viruses. We have the determination and ability to handle these social problems.   2005

ON HIMSELF AND HIS FAMILY

I had 25 divisions to choose from when the PAP nominated me to stand for elections. I chose Tanjong Pagar. The people of Tanjong Pagar have a right to know why. Tanjong Pagar is a working-class area. No other division has such a high proportion of workers, wage earners, small traders and such a low proportion of wealthy merchants and landlords living in it. I wanted to represent the workers, wage earners and small traders, not wealthy merchants or landlords. So I chose Tanjong Pagar, not Tanglin.　　　1955

I have been accused of many things in my life, but not even my worst enemy has ever accused me of being afraid to speak my mind.　　　1955

I was sent to an English school to equip me to go to an English university in order that I could then be an educated man – the equal of any Englishman – the model of perfection! I do not know how far they have succeeded in that. I grew up, and finally graduated. At the end of it, I felt – and it was long before I entered politics, in fact it is one of the reasons why I am here – that the whole set of values was wrong, fundamentally and radically wrong.　　　1956

When I read Nehru[10] – and I read a lot of Nehru – I understood him when he said, 'I cry when I think that I cannot speak my own mother tongue as well as I can speak the English language'. I am a less emotional man, I do not usually cry, or tear my hair, or tear paper, or tear my shirt off, but that does not mean that I feel any the less strongly about it.　　　1956

If my responsibilities could be measured only by the salary I am paid, I think I could find much more congenial pursuits besides having to discharge the duties of my office. 1964

———⊂⊙⊃———

I am prepared to take chances with my life. That is one thing. Only I will be sorry for it and maybe [my] immediate family. But I am not prepared to take chances with the lives of two million people. 1965

———⊂⊙⊃———

Rest on laurels? I wish I could do that. No, you rest when you're dead. 1978

———⊂⊙⊃———

When my senior Cabinet colleagues and I look back on our early hectic years of governing Singapore, we realise how much we have benefited from having gone through a very hard school. We met street thugs, not street urchins. Had we not become streetwise we would have been clobbered. Like dogs which are closeted in a bungalow behind fences, we would have been run over when exposed to treacherous traffic. 1984

———⊂⊙⊃———

Even a great figure in history, like Winston Churchill, was unceremoniously bundled out of office in July 1945, and after fighting and winning a great war from 1940–1945. I am therefore thankful that Singaporeans, by supporting the PAP in the 8th General Election since 1959, have allowed me to choose the manner and circumstance in which I shall leave office. 1988

———⊂⊙⊃———

And even from my sickbed, even if you are going to lower me into the grave and I feel that something is going wrong … I'll get up! 1988

When I visited Madame Tussaud's as a student in the 1940s at Baker Street, London, there were two groups of figures: the famous and the notorious, either British kings and famous leaders, or notorious murderers. I hope Madame Tussaud's will not put my likeness too close to the notorious.   1998

———

The three and a half years of Japanese occupation were the most important of my life. They gave me vivid insights into the behaviour of human beings and human societies, their motivations and impulses. My appreciation of governments, my understanding of power as the vehicle for revolutionary change, would not have been gained without this experience.   1998

———

My speeches in this House [Parliament of Singapore] mirrored the changes in mood and challenge of the time. The first two years (1955 to about 1957), I was light-hearted and enjoyed the cut and thrust of parliamentary debate. When I had to compete against the communists for grassroots support, and realised how deep and all-embracing was their grip on the ground and their determination to seize power, my mood changed. I lost my youthful innocence.   1999

———

I always tried to be correct, not politically correct.   2000

———

I was never a prisoner of any theory. What guided me were reason and reality. The acid test I applied to every theory or scheme was, would it work?
     2000

I have had to sing four national anthems: Britain's *God Save the Queen*, Japan's *Kimigayo*, Malaysia's *Negara Ku*, and finally Singapore's *Majulah Singapura*; such were the political upheavals of the last 60 years. 2000

—◦—

At the end of the day, what I cherish most are the human relationships. With the unfailing support of my wife and partner I have lived my life to the fullest. It is the friendships I made and the close family ties I nurtured that have provided me with that sense of satisfaction at a life well lived, and have made me what I am. 2003

—◦—

We run a meritocracy. If the Lee family sets an example of nepotism, that system collapses. If I were not the Prime Minister, he [Lee Hsien Loong] could have become Prime Minister several years earlier. It is against my interest to allow any family member, who's incapable, to be holding an important job because that would be a disaster for Singapore and my legacy. That cannot be allowed. 2005

—◦—

Do you believe for one moment that my son [Prime Minister Lee Hsien Loong], and before him Goh Chok Tong, my son is 53 years old, 54 coming on to, hasn't a mind of his own, he needs me to whisper how to answer, how to plan the future? He didn't need me to decide his career, he chose to join the SAF [Singapore Armed Forces] on his own, he chose to go into politics on his own, discussing it with Goh Chok Tong, who was Minister for Defence. He asked me. I said, 'Think it over carefully'. In '84 he had just lost his wife; Wong died in '82. I said, 'You're going to make it very difficult for yourself, getting another wife,' because he had two young children. This is not a joke. We are not running this for ourselves. If we were, Singapore wouldn't be what it is. 2006

We [Madame Kwa Geok Choo[4] and Lee Kuan Yew] gradually influenced each other's ways and habits, we adjusted and accommodated each other. We knew that we could not stay starry-eyed lovers all our lives, that life was an ever-ongoing challenge. With new problems to resolve and manage.   2010

———◦∞◦———

Without her [Madame Kwa Geok Choo] I would have been a different man, [with] a completely different life.   2010

CHRONOLOGY

1923: Lee Kuan Yew born in Singapore

1942: Three and a half year Japanese occupation of Singapore begins

1947: Lee Kuan Yew and Kwa Geok Choo secretly marry in London

1949: Lee Kuan Yew awarded his law degree

1950: Lee Kuan Yew and Kwa Geok Choo celebrate a second wedding ceremony in Singapore

1954: The People's Action Party (PAP) is founded by Lee Kuan Yew and a group of like-minded, anti-colonial individuals

1955: Lee Kuan Yew elected as MP for Tanjong Pagar

Hock Lee riots occur due to trade union disputes

1957: Britain agrees to Singapore's self-rule

1959: Lee Kuan Yew is sworn in as Prime Minister of a self-governing Singapore

1963: Singapore declares independence from Britain, before formation of the Federation of Malaysia

The Federation of Malaysia, including Malaya, Singapore, Sarawak and Sabah, is formed

1964: Communal riots erupt in Singapore

1965: Singapore separates from Federation of Malaysia and becomes an independent republic

1967: Singapore becomes a founder member of the Association of Southeast Asian Nations (ASEAN)

1968: Britain announces intent to withdraw all military forces from Singapore in 1971

1981: J B Jeyaretnam wins by-election in the Anson constituency to become the first opposition MP since independence

1988: Group Representation Constituency (GRC) scheme comes into effect

1990: Lee Kuan Yew steps down from position of Prime Minister after 31 years, remains a cabinet member in the position of Senior Minister

Goh Chok Tong sworn in as Prime Minister

1997: Asian financial crisis begins

2004: Lee Hsien Loong sworn in as Prime Minister

Lee Kuan Yew becomes Minister Mentor

2011: Lee Kuan Yew steps down as Minister Mentor but remains MP for Tanjong Pagar

2015: Lee Kuan Yew passed away on 23 March at Singapore General Hospital

ENDNOTES

1 Merdeka is the Malay expression used to refer to independence.

2 Tunku Abdul Rahman was Malaysia's first prime minister, from 1957 to 1970.

3 This quote is taken from the Proclamation of Singapore.

4 Madame Kwa Geok Choo was Lee Kuan Yew's wife.

5 J B Jeyaretnam was the leader of the Workers' Party, from 1971 to 2001.

6 The Strangers' Gallery is the area designated to the public in Parliament.

7 Deng Xiaoping was China's 'paramount leader', from 1978 to 1992.

8 RTS (Radio Television Singapore) is now MediaCorp.

9 SEATO was a defence pact between some Asian countries (though not Singapore) and certain Western countries during the Cold War.

10 Jawaharlal Nehru was the first prime minister of India, from 1947 to 1964.

11 A *hui guan* is a Chinese clan association.

PUBLISHER'S ACKNOWLEDGEMENTS

Most of the quotations in this book were selected from STARS, the Speech-Text Archival and Retrieval System maintained online by the National Archives of Singapore. This invaluable online resource contains the speeches of government Ministers and Presidents, as well as press releases and government reports. Editions Didier Millet wishes to thank the National Archives of Singapore for creating this resource, which can be accessed via http://a2o.nas.sg/stars.

Another important source of quotations was the Singapore Parliament Reports, which contains a verbatim record of each sitting. It can be accessed via http://www.parliament.gov.sg/publications-singapore-parliament-reports.

Editions Didier Millet is grateful to Marshall Cavendish for permission to use excerpts from *The Singapore Story* (1998) and *From Third World to First: The Singapore Story 1965–2000* (2000). These excerpts were 14c, 14d, 21d, 32c, 35a, 48e, 53b, 69c, 69d, 111d, 156b, 156c, 159b, 159d, 159e and 160a.

The book's manuscript was reviewed by Professor Chan Heng Chee, whose comments and suggestions were invaluable.

Editions Didier Millet would like to thank SR Nathan and Anthony Tan for their help in facilitating this project.

Lastly, we would like to thank Mr Lee Kuan Yew for kindly agreeing to the publication of this anthology of quotations.